ANCESTRAL
Magic

ANCESTRAL Magic

Empower the here and now with enchanting guidance from your past family history

Kirsten Riddle

Illustrated by Gina Rosas Moncada

CICO BOOKS

LONDON NEW YORK

Published in 2023 by CICO Books
An imprint of Ryland Peters & Small Ltd

20–21 Jockey's Fields   341 E 116th St
London WC1R 4BW   New York, NY 10029

www.rylandpeters.com

10 9 8 7 6 5 4 3 2 1

A CIP catalog record for this book is available from the Library of Congress and the British Library.

ISBN: 978-1-80065-261-3

Printed in China

Editor: Caroline West
Illustrator: Gina Rosas Moncada

Commissioning editor: Kristine Pidkameny
Senior designer: Emily Breen
Art director: Sally Powell
Creative director: Leslie Harrington
Production manager: Gordana Simakovic
Publishing manager: Penny Craig
Publisher: Cindy Richards

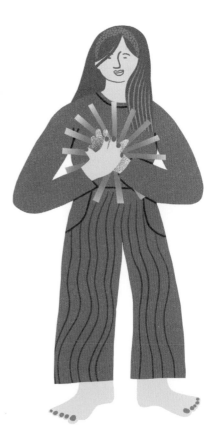

CONTENTS

INTRODUCTION

Ancestral Magic is everywhere. It is in every moment of every day because it's in you. It doesn't matter what your age or background is, or the kind of person you are. Even if you don't believe in anything mystical, you can still feel the effects of Ancestral Magic at work. It's in the way you walk and the way you talk, in your accent, attitude, and the way you interact with people. It's in the stories you tell yourself and others, and the patterns that you weave into your life. It's in the little things that you do without thought or recognition, like the way you laugh, or your ability to empathize when others would simply walk away. It's also in the much bigger rituals that have come to mean something to you and your family, in those things you do when you get together to mark the occasion and the stories you share time and again because it is tradition.

Ancestral Magic is in the superstitions you create and the heirlooms you carry as good luck charms. For example, when you purposely wear your grandma's ring to an important meeting, you do it because you want to feel connected to her in some way, to be imbued with her

strength and energy. This makes you feel confident and able to deal with anything that comes your way. Even the cynics among us would admit that having roots to secure you can make all the difference to how you feel at any given time. Knowing where you come from and a little about those connections can help you recognize your true worth and discover the gifts and talents that you have been given. And the good news is, we all have the potential to feel a sense of belonging. We all have ancestors. You may know nothing about them except that they existed and helped to bring you into the world, and that is enough because the answers reside within you. You are the first port of call when it comes to working with Ancestral Magic.

Your DNA is unique and made up of all those people who went before, so you are innately linked to them, and this is the key. By going within and learning to trust your intuition and listen to your higher self, you'll strengthen those bonds and unite with their power. Combine this with a little fact-finding, sharing tales with your nearest and dearest, and listening to the things they want to tell you, and you will soon re-establish those connections. You'll unlock the secrets of the past and even receive spiritual guidance from lost loved ones in spirit.

This book is a starting point from which you can explore Ancestral Magic. It introduces you to the concept and provides rituals and suggestions that will help you tap into your familial power. You'll learn techniques to heighten your psychic abilities and help you connect with your ancestral guides, along with ways you can feel more empowered and protected. You will learn how to create affirmations and talismans to generate positive energy and attract abundance, and you'll also discover the healing power of ancestral karma and what it means for you. The book combines practical exercises with more spiritual pursuits like meditation and visualization to help you on your journey, but most importantly, the activities within these pages are fun. They're meant to get you talking and sharing, to encourage the flow of communication, so that you also strengthen your existing relationships. If you follow the suggestions within each chapter, you should learn something about yourself and those close to you. After all, family is at the heart of everything, and understanding what makes them tick will also help you understand your own attitudes and beliefs, and where they come from.

Ancestral Magic is personal and different for everyone. It's up to you how far you want to take it, and if you want to delve deeper and actually get into the nitty gritty of tracing your family tree and unlocking the secrets of your DNA (which are not covered here), then this is a good starting point since it puts you in the right spiritual mindset. It helps you recognize the importance of the past, and how it shapes the present and the future. It also hones your intuitive skills and gives you the confidence to follow your heart and be who you were meant to be. You'll boost your personal power and be able to take what you learn with you, into every area of your life. After all, you'll have a spiritual tag-team of ancestors who you can call upon whenever you need them.

So enjoy, explore, and follow your own path. Make room for your ancestors and set a place for them at your table. Welcome them into your world and open your heart to their wisdom. In doing so, you'll unleash your Ancestral Magic and truly shine!

What's in a Name?

This chapter looks at the importance of connecting with your ancestors and how this can help you. It outlines the tools you might need along the way to do this, as well as how to create those spiritual links with the past. It highlights the importance of knowing who you are and where you come from, and shows you how to draw those initial comparisons to get you started on your unique journey. You will also discover more about yourself and how connecting with your ancestors can help you identify your true purpose.

"The past and present
unite in me."

Ancestral Magic Toolkit

Working with your ancestors is a journey, and like any great expedition, you will need supplies and tools to help you navigate a path. What you need may change, depending on the work you're doing, but there will always be key items that can help you connect and work with Ancestral Magic. Here's a checklist of things to get you started.

Ancestral Magic Journal

Reflection is a key part of working with your ancestors. Being able to note down thoughts and feelings, and any insights you receive, in one place is important. You will be able to look back and see the progress you have made. You can use the journal to document your feelings and also to write down any intuitive messages you receive. You can also use it as a creative outlet. Connecting with the spirits of lost loved ones and working with Ancestral Magic requires a degree of imagination and the ability to flex your creative muscles. Your journal is a safe place where you can do this. You can give your imagination free reign and tap into inner wisdom, and it doesn't matter what you write, as this is solely for you.

Meditation Mat or Cushion

You will find a selection of mindful meditations, guided visualizations, and breathing exercises in this book. These activities are designed to help you open a doorway to the past. They allow your subconscious mind to take control, so you can access inner wisdom and connect with the voices of the past. It makes sense, therefore, to have a safe and comfortable space where you can perform these exercises. Having a special mat or cushion where you can sit helps to create the right atmosphere. It's a trigger for the subconscious, which says, "Now I am going to be still and go within." It puts you in the right mindset to approach any of the activities because you know that the minute you position the mat/cushion and sit on it, you are going to be working with Ancestral Magic.

Photographs of Family Members

Old photographs are a powerful addition to your Ancestral Magic toolkit. They provide a portal into the past. They're a snapshot of a moment in time and a way to connect with any ancestor. Just by taking in the appearance and expression of your ancestors, you will learn a lot about them. It doesn't matter if you have never met the person, as having a picture of them in front of you will help to focus your mind and any magical intentions you have. To prepare for the exercises ahead, gather together as many old family photographs as you can find.

Mementoes and Heirlooms

In most families, you will find treasured heirlooms or mementoes linked to special memories. There is sometimes family lore associated with these items, but the value of others might be more personal to you. An item you inherit is particularly powerful. It's a link to the past and something that was once cherished by a member of your family line.

Mirror

Mirrors capture your reflection and give you a space to focus on, which can help when you're trying to connect with the energy of lost loved ones. A mirror can also give you a focal point to fix on when you're meditating, or you can use it as a scrying tool to access your subconscious mind (more on this later in the book). When you gaze at a mirror and look into your eyes, you are in effect looking into your soul, which is ultimately tied to all the other souls in your family group. You carry the wisdom of your ancestors with you, and mirror work can be the key to unlocking this treasure trove of knowledge.

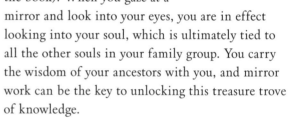

Candles

Ceremony is an important part of Ancestral Magic. The rituals you create when you need to speak with your ancestors and seek their guidance are incredibly important, as is creating the right atmosphere. Candles can help you do this. They help to focus the mind, and each hue has different properties, depending on what you're looking for. For example, if you're seeking wisdom from the past, you might choose to light a purple candle because this is associated with intuition and inner knowledge. If you're looking to your ancestors for strength and confidence, you might light a red candle to help you feel assertive and empowered.

Candle Color Guide

White — Healing, calming, peace

Silver — Cleansing, psychic perception

Gold — Connecting with your higher self

Pink — Love, beauty, self-esteem

Red — Power, confidence, asserting yourself

Blue — Emotional healing

Green — Connection with the natural world, abundance

Yellow — Creativity, self-expression

Orange — Happiness, positive energy

Purple — Wisdom, intuition

Brown — Grounding, security

Black — Protection, balance

Crystals

Crystals are powerful stones; they resonate with energy and can magnify and transmit your intentions through the ether. They are healing too, which makes them the perfect fit for Ancestral Magic. Much of the work you do will involve looking into inherited patterns of behavior and karma, and crystals can help with this. They can also bring clarity and boost your intuition. Some crystals will unlock your subconscious, while others will stimulate creativity. There are so many to choose from, depending on what you need and what you hope to achieve, but if you are only going to have one in your toolkit, then opt for a piece of clear quartz. This stone is a good all-rounder: it helps to transmit energy, improve your psychic perception, and boost healing.

Crystal Guide

Amethyst	Unlocks the Third Eye chakra and boosts psychic perception
Black tourmaline	Grounds and protects, while cleansing your energy
Fluorite	Enhances mental abilities and brings clarity
Jasper	Balances yin yang energy, and heightens psychic perception
Labradorite	Enhances communication with the spiritual realm
Lapis lazuli	Helps tap into ancient knowledge
Moonstone	Calms and soothes the emotions, while improving intuition
Obsidian	Helps to combat fear, strengthens spiritual connections
Opal	Helps you tune into inner wisdom and heightens sensitivity
Selenite	Protects and cleanses, while strengthening spiritual connections

Identify Your Goals

Before you begin working with your ancestors, it's a good idea to identify your specific needs and aims. What do you hope to achieve by connecting with the past? Spend some time pondering this question. You might have a number of different aims. For instance, you may be looking for a sense of belonging, a way to feel anchored and strong in the present moment. Maybe you're looking for spiritual guidance from your ancestors or just want to learn more about them and their stories. Perhaps your interest is more general, and you simply want to see what surfaces when you begin digging deeper, or maybe you're using this journey to develop your intuitive gifts.

Spend time reflecting on your needs and aims, then write a list of these in your journal. Highlight the ones that are most important to you. Once you have identified them, you can perform a simple ritual to set your spiritual intention. This will put you in the right mindset and help to solidify your aims, which serves to motivate you on your journey.

TRY THIS!
Set Your Intention

As with any ritual, it's important to set aside time and space, as well as to create the right atmosphere.

1. To begin, light a white candle and burn some frankincense essential oil in an oil burner. If you prefer, you can anoint the candle with a few drops of the essential oil before lighting it. Frankincense is associated with your higher self and will help to raise your energy vibration and boost psychic perception.

2. Spend a few minutes focusing on the flame. Watch how it grows in width and length, going from strength to strength. Imagine there's a tiny flame sitting in your belly. Each time you inhale, the flame becomes more powerful—feel it extend upward to fill your chest with warmth and light. As you exhale, you release any negative energy that you have been holding onto. See this as a trail of smoke that leaves your body with each outward breath.

3. Hold your journal in front of you and read out loud the list of aims you wrote down.

4. Say, "These are my intentions, the goals that I have set. May my spirit align with my subconscious mind, to help me on my journey. May my ancestors light the way and hold out their hands, so that I may connect with them and know myself better. As I have spoken, so it shall be. My intention is clear and important to me."

5. Now spend a few minutes breathing in the peace that surrounds you.

Who Are You?

This might seem like a strange question. After all, you already know who you are. You were born into a family, and over time you grew and learned about yourself and the world around you. You made friends and connections, had good and bad experiences, and responded in your own way. You developed qualities, traits, and opinions, which helped you make sense of your environment and interact with others. You, more than anyone, know what makes you tick. But while you implicitly know certain things about your character and personality, what would you discover if you decided to dig a little deeper? Is there a side to you that you keep hidden from others? Maybe you're not even aware of it yourself. There are so many facets to your personality, some of which have been learned through experience and some that are inherent to who you are. Talents can also lay dormant for years, and it is only in a moment of madness, or realization, that they come to the fore. Imagine being able to delve into the heart of who you are and what really matters to you—you might discover a special ability that is unique to you and your family. You could widen your skill set, and you'd certainly learn more about yourself and those close to you.

When we ask the question "Who are you?" it's easy to scrape the surface and believe that what we see and experience is everything there is. But you are not alone in this world; you are the result of generations of family who have gone before. And while their experiences of the world might have been very different from your own, they are still a part of you. They have shaped and created who you are today. Their unique DNA forms a trail that leads to you, which means they live on in you, in some small way.

Imagine that you could have an audience with just one of your many ancestors. What might you discover about yourself in the process? Even if you only asked a handful of questions, you would learn something about who they were and how they lived. Now imagine asking the same questions of yourself. What would your response be, and how would it define you as a person? What kind of picture would you create for the ones who come after you? To really know who you are, you need to see things from a different perspective, look below the surface, and consider not only what went before, but also what is to come and what you hope to leave behind.

TRY THIS!

Past, Present, Future

1. Sit with your journal and spend a few moments in quiet reflection. Breathe deeply and calm your mind. Release any stress that you are holding in your body and simply enjoy a moment of peace with yourself.

2. Write three headings at the top of a page: "Past," "Present," and "Future."

3. Now ask yourself the question "Who am I?" beneath each of these headings. In other words, who were you in the past, who are you right now, and who will you be in the future?

4. Allow yourself some time to ponder this question in relation to all three stages of your life. Breathe deeply and let the thoughts flow in your mind.

5. How you choose to answer is entirely up to you. You can write a few sentences or a brief description, or, if you prefer, jot down key words to summarize. You might even want to draw a picture or write a poem; the choice is yours. Allowing your creativity to flow can help you connect with the questions at a deeper level.

6. Once you have put something under each heading, take a moment to reflect. Look at what you have written. You may notice some changes as you have evolved from past to present, or perhaps you hope to make some changes for your future self; you may also notice some similarities. There may be qualities you would like to develop for your future self and qualities that you feel you have left behind. All the things you have written are relevant because they are a part of your makeup.

7. Acknowledge that you are more than just your present self: you are the person you were and the person you will become. Once you begin to understand this, you'll get a deeper insight into who you are, and this will also help you look at your ancestors in a different way. They may appear to be one thing on the surface, but, just like you, they evolved and changed. What they left behind as a legacy is just one part of who they were. They went through many stages to reach that place.

8. To finish, say this affirmation: "I am the sum of all my parts: my past, my present, and my future."

Make Connections

When you want to connect spiritually with your ancestors, one of the best places to start is with yourself. After all, you carry a part of them within you, so it makes sense that you hold the key to unlocking the past. It's all about making connections, looking at yourself and your life, and following the threads back in time. You have already identified what you'd like to achieve, and you have also considered who you are and who you would like to be. Now it's time to make those connections. You can do this in a number of ways. Asking questions of your nearest and dearest might shed some light on lost loved ones and recent ancestors. Using your intuition, through meditation and visualization, will also help. There are a number of techniques you can use to glean information and connect with the past. Think of yourself as a detective, piecing together clues and following loose threads. To get you started, there are some practical suggestions on the following pages.

"I am shaped and molded by many generations."

Follow the Threads

To begin making connections with your past, start with what you know about your ancestors, from things you have been told by current family members to any photographs you have seen. Even if you haven't got any pictures to help you connect, consider the relatives you know right now and bring them to mind.

Physical

Look for physical resemblances: are there any distinguishing features within your family? Consider height, build, coloring, and facial characteristics. Look for those physical ties that bind you together. These recurring factors have come from somewhere along your family line; they are the result of those who went before and will give you an impression of what some of your ancestors may have looked like. If you're lucky to have a selection of old photographs, you'll be able to see these similarities yourself, but even without them, you can still make a fairly good guess at what features you have inherited and draw a link between you and your ancestors.

Emotional

Look for an emotional resonance with your ancestors. What kind of people were they? How would they have coped with different challenges? Again, you can ask questions within your family. You will probably have a good idea of qualities and traits that you have inherited from immediate family members, but try and go back further. Imagine what life was like for your great-grandparents or their parents before them. Consider the times they lived in and the challenges they would have faced. Look for those emotional clues, the things you do now, that you might have inherited. Yes, it's partly guesswork, but this is where you need to trust your intuition and follow your instincts. The threads will be there. Consider any stories you know about your relatives, the ones that really resonate with you and make you feel emotional. It is likely that you share an emotional link with this ancestor, at some level. Look for the similarities between you.

Spiritual

Consider the spiritual links that you share with the past. Do you feel an intuitive connection to any of your ancestors? Perhaps there's a more recent relative that you remember, and who you feel spiritually tied to. This may be because you have something in common, or it could be more subtle—maybe their energy is aligned with your own. This is something you will know instinctively. Look to your dreams for direction. For example, you might have a recurring dream featuring a lost loved one. This is a spiritual connection: they are speaking to you through your subconscious mind, while your conscious mind is asleep. Perhaps there is an ancestor who stands out for you. You never met them, but you keep thinking about them and feel their presence around you. This is also a spiritual connection.

TRY THIS!
Create a Family Collage

While you might not be sure who your ancestors were, there's no harm in flexing your creative muscles and creating a family collage. This is a fun exercise that taps into your imagination and also helps to cement your spiritual connection to the past.

1. Look to your links with the past, considering the physical, emotional, and spiritual ties that you have established. What have you discovered so far? While you might not know the truth with absolute accuracy, you will have made some assumptions, which can help you build a clearer picture.
2. Start by placing yourself in the center of the picture in some way. You could use a photo, a drawing, or a symbol to represent who you are. It's entirely up to you.
3. Now add any relatives using an artistic representation of who they are in your life. Draw lines between you to show your connection.
4. Next consider what you know about your ancestors. If you have information about specific people, you could try adding this, or if you just have a few ideas of what they might have been like, you could include pictures, symbols, and sketches to represent these. For example, if you think your ancestors worked on the land, planting and farming, you could include a picture of a farmer or crops growing in a field, along with a short description or their name. How you represent your ancestors is up to you; it's more important to be creative.
5. Think about the physical connections your made in the previous exercise. For instance, if you think your ancestors probably had dark hair and eyes, include this in your collage.

6. Consider the emotional links too. For example, if you know you come from a temperamental, artistic family, find a way to represent this with a picture or symbol.
7. When you have finished, place your collage somewhere you will see it every day. This will re-enforce your connection with the past and your ancestors.
8. Remember too that you can change or add to the collage at any point. It's an evolving picture and a representation of your past and present.

YOU WILL NEED

Large piece of paper or card, colored pens and pencils, pictures from magazines, glue, and any crafty supplies you may want for decoration

Listen and Learn

Ancestral Magic relies on a degree of research, on you taking the initiative and finding out as much as you can about your ancestors. While you might not have time to conduct an in-depth search for your family history, you can glean as much information as possible from relatives and family friends. All you need is a little time to ask some questions, and then to listen and learn. Write up your findings because, even if you think you'll remember everything, it's a good idea to make notes that you can refer to. Treat this as a research project, and put in the time and effort. Record conversations. Encourage those who knew your parents/grandparents/great-grandparents to tell stories and share their memories. It is from these simple moments that you will not only discover important links to the past, but also cement those links through the people who are still here and a part of your life.

"My identity is made up of many voices."

Meditate on Your True Purpose

Your ancestors want you to succeed, and they can empower and nourish you on your journey. Learning about them, from them, and with them will help you identify your true purpose and re-enforce your sense of self. Connecting with them spiritually will trigger your intuition and strengthen those skills. You'll become more self-aware and learn to trust your instincts. To help with this, make meditation a key part of your practice.

"I learn from the wisdom
of my ancestors."

TRY THIS!

Thread of Light

1. Find somewhere comfortable to sit. Roll your shoulders back and lengthen your spine. Imagine a thread of light emerging from the top of your head. Feel it tugging upward gently as you stretch and extend your chest.
2. Close your eyes and take a long, deep breath in through the nose. As you exhale, release any stress or tension. Continue to breathe in this way for a couple of minutes.
3. When you're ready, bring your attention back to the top of your head. Visualize the thread of light traveling upward. Know that it connects you with the Universe.
4. Follow the path of the thread as it soars above your head and into the heavens. Imagine it flowing back in time, back to those who went before. At some point, the thread splits in many different directions, connecting you with your ancestors.
5. As you breathe in, you strengthen this connection and the light becomes brighter as the energy flows between you.
6. As you breathe out, you release any fear or doubt. Continue to visualize a beam of light traveling along the thread, back through the top of your head as you inhale.
7. Enjoy the strength of this connection and feel the joyful energy that it brings to your body, mind, and soul.
8. Every time your mind wanders, bring your focus back to the light and your breathing.
9. Know that this simple meditation can help you connect with your ancestors, at any time. It can help you feel strong and energized, and if you need help or guidance, it can provide a spiritual link to your ancestors.

Other Ways to Get to Know Your True Self

Get a deeper understanding of what makes you tick with these simple suggestions that you can incorporate into your daily life.

Record Your Dreams

Get into the habit of leaving a notebook and pen by your bed. Each night before you go to sleep, do a breathing exercise to calm your mind, then when you're ready, ask your subconscious to speak to you in a dream. If you're looking for specific answers, then ask any relevant questions. If you'd just like to strengthen your connection to the past and flex your intuition, ask for a meaningful dream to help you. You won't always receive the answers you seek, but performing a ritual and setting this intention will encourage insightful dreams.

Go Back to Your Youth

What did you enjoy doing as a child? Take a step back in time and ask yourself this question. Bring to mind memories of childhood play. What were your favorite games? Did you have a dream, or perhaps you always wanted to do or be something, like a detective or an artist? Your hopes and dreams when you were a child can help you understand who you really are and what motivates you. Even if you haven't acted upon these things, it's not too late. Ask yourself what appealed to you then, and why? If you liked making up stories, and you had a vivid imagination, do you still use it? Are you flexing those creative muscles today? If not, is there something you can do to help you access that side of your personality? To truly know yourself and your roots, you need to go back as far as you can, to the core of your psyche.

The Shape of Your Name

Get up close and personal with your name. It is often the first thing that people see or hear about you, and it helps to shape your identity, but what does it mean to you and how does it define you? Try the following exercise.

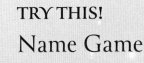

TRY THIS!

Name Game

1. Think about your first name and what it means to you. Do you like it? Do you like to be called by your name, or do you prefer a nickname, and if so, why?
2. Now bring to mind your family name. What does it make you think of? Do you associate certain qualities with this name?
3. Make a list of these qualities, writing down the first things that come to mind.
4. Close your eyes and let your mind wander. Let the images come and go, and if any stand out, make a note of them.
5. Are there any names in your family history that resonate with you? Even if you know nothing about the person, their name might strike a chord with you. It might create a picture and help you connect with that ancestor.
6. If you can, draw a picture or create a description of the person, just from their name. It doesn't matter if this doesn't match what the individual looked like, as this is about connecting with their energy.

Get Talking

Talk to your parents and other relatives and friends who knew you as a child, and ask them what you were like. Have you changed much? Do they see a difference in you now? Have they noticed a family resemblance in the way you behave? Asking questions can help you create a sense of self and a link to the past. You might be reminded of gifts that you've forgotten about, and sharing memories in this way will strengthen the bonds with your nearest and dearest. It will also help you reconnect with your inner child and experience the playful joy of your youth again.

"I carry those who went before in my heart and mind."

Journal Exercise

Think about what you have learned in this chapter. What have you discovered about yourself and how does it feel to strengthen your connection with the past? Do you feel differently about who you are? If so, why? What can you take from this, to help you feel more self-assured? Perhaps you have discovered a different side to your personality that you would like to explore. Think about the ways you can do this and the actions you might take. Also think about what you know so far about your ancestors. Can you see links forming between you? These connections could be similarities that you have identified, both emotional and physical, or just a deeper understanding of how their life might have been.

Highlight three things you have discovered while reading and performing the exercises in this chapter. These can be simple things, such as a love of dancing that you had as a child, which you'd like to reignite as an adult, or a similarity in your build and coloring that connects you with your ancestors.

What Your Ancestors Want You to Know

This chapter highlights the different ways you can communicate with your ancestors in the spiritual realm. It offers an insight into each technique and shows you how it can be used to begin those conversations. It provides a starting point from which you can explore these significant relationships and receive the guidance and healing that your ancestors wish to send you. Communication is a two-way process, so you will learn not only how to get their attention and start the conversation, but also how to listen for the signs and messages they have for you.

"My ancestral guides
watch over me."

Conversations with Your Ancestors

If you could talk to any one of your ancestors right now, what would you say? You would probably have lots of questions for them. Maybe you want to ask for advice or guidance in a particular area, or perhaps you would be happy to simply sit and listen to anything they had to say. After all, they have a wealth of experience that you can draw upon.

It's inevitable that they would want to help you and pass on some of their wisdom and healing energy. When we pass on to the next realm, we too are making a spiritual journey. We become more enlightened and have the opportunity to help those we have left behind, whether that's by steering them in the right direction or sending powerful healing to help them create positive energy.

Your ancestors will want to do this for you, to connect in whatever way they can, even if you're not fully aware of it. It must be extremely frustrating at times when it seems that we don't hear what they have to say or pick up on the subtle clues they send us. Of course, we cannot be blamed for this. In a world of ten thousand things, it's easy to get sidetracked and stifle intuition, and instead focus on the superficial. Spirits speak through our subconscious. They send us signs through the power of synchronicity. They want to have a conversation with us, so how can we communicate with them and receive their insights?

You can use a range of psychic tools to meet your ancestors and have these exchanges. From visualization, giving your imagination free reign and allowing intuition to take control, to meditation, which strengthens your connection with the spiritual realm and your higher self. Then there are more practical pursuits like actively seeking clues, learning to be open to synchronicity, and connecting through memory work.

However you have these conversations is up to you, but one thing is certain: they will enhance your life and help you navigate a path through the world. They will give you a sense of belonging, an inner strength, and a way of accessing ancestral wisdom that will help in all you do. You will also receive spiritual healing from your ancestors. By inviting them into your world, you open the channels of communication and allow the healing energy to flow, which will boost your vitality and help you recharge when you're feeling vulnerable.

Synchronicity

The power of synchronicity is at work in your life every day, even if you're not fully aware of it. While you might assume that something is a delightful coincidence, synchronicity is much more potent than this. It is about a group of events or occurrences, sent from the Universe and the spiritual realm to provide guidance or deliver a specific message. Often reassuring and life-affirming, synchronicity tells you that you are on the right path; it provides a moment of enlightenment and is most likely meaningful in a personal way. This is how you know the difference between synchronicity and coincidence: it feels much bigger and more significant when it happens. It's as if spiritual forces have combined to send a message, something that cannot easily be ignored. That said, synchronicity doesn't have to be a bolt from the blue. It can be something simple like a powerful song lyric that you keep hearing, and which resonates with you. The spirit world often uses synchronicity to get your attention, and it is one clear way that your ancestors will speak to you. If you are hoping to connect with them, then it's important to be aware of this process and how it works.

The key, as with any form of spiritual communication, is to be open and present. To tune into the world, rather than out of it. To be aware and interested in everything, rather than being bogged down with worry or stress, and to take time to listen to your intuition. It's important to notice when things pique your interest. We often ignore signs from spirit because we are busy ticking things off our own "to do" list. By practicing some of the techniques within this chapter, you will naturally align yourself with synchronicity. You'll hone your intuition and be more open to those communications that come from your ancestors.

TRY THIS!
Physical Triggers

1. Your intuition can help you establish when synchronicity is at work and also decipher messages from your ancestors. The key is to read the physical signs that you receive and to trust your instincts.
2. You can do this by becoming more aware of what your body is telling you. For example, when something good happens, which is both exciting and unexpected, notice how your body reacts. Do you get butterflies in the pit of your stomach, or perhaps a tingling sensation along your spine? The same goes for ominous events—perhaps you get a heavy dragging feeling in your stomach or you feel the pressure in some other way.
3. Identify your key physical triggers and be aware of what they mean to you. Learn to trust these feelings and let your intuition guide you. You might want to make a note of what they are and when you feel them, then see what happens afterward and whether your assumptions were correct.
4. As you become more aware of spiritual signs and synchronicities, and learn to trust your intuition, you'll instinctively know when your ancestors are sending you a sign or guiding you in a particular direction.

"The voices of my ancestors guide and nurture me."

Visualization

This is a powerful practice that can strengthen your intuition and help you connect with your ancestors in the spiritual realm. Visualization involves picturing a scenario and letting it play out in your mind, rather like putting yourself in the center of the action in a movie. You are the lead character and you have creative control. You can go anywhere and do anything in a visualization. You can be anything you want; it's about allowing yourself to daydream and picture events as they unfold.

Visualization can be used to create positive energy and manifest the future, by controlling your thoughts. You see what you want to happen and act as if it has already happened. By reaffirming this over and over again, you send a powerful message to the Universe and generate positive energy. In the same way, visualization can help you connect with spiritual realms. You are engaging your subconscious mind, which allows your intuition to flow. Each time you let your imagination take over, you are tapping into an otherworldly source of energy and opening up a window into another dimension with your psychic senses. Each time you do this, the veil between this world and the next becomes thinner, and you are able to communicate with those in spirit.

TRY THIS!

The Staircase Method

Find somewhere comfortable that you can sit and won't be disturbed. Visualization takes time, and you don't want to be rushed or interrupted mid-flow. You can create a relaxing atmosphere by burning scented candles and playing some soothing background music.

1. When you are ready spend a couple of minutes focusing on your breathing. Draw a deep breath in, counting four long beats, then do the same thing as you exhale. Continue this breathing cycle and then extend the breath counts to five. You should begin to feel more relaxed after a couple of minutes.

2. Close your eyes and imagine you are looking at a winding staircase. It leads down somewhere deep below. You can see the gentle glow of light in the distance; it looks warm and inviting.

3. Slowly you begin to descend the staircase, counting out the rhythm of your steps in a "one, two" pattern. The farther you go, the calmer you feel. Your body is relaxed, your mind is still, and the only sound is the soft rhythm of your breathing and the tapping of your footsteps.

4. Eventually the staircase ends and you reach the lower level. You can see a corridor up ahead, with several doors. Each door leads to a room and one of your ancestors. They are all gathered to meet you.

5. Take your time and walk down the corridor, noticing how the doors are decorated. Perhaps they are painted different colors or have numbers or names on them. Let your imagination take over and provide the detail.

6. You will probably find that you are drawn to one room more than the others. Take your time, knock on the door, and enter. Give yourself time to acclimatize to the room. What can you see? Is it big or small? Are there any windows? Is it empty? Perhaps it's fully furnished in a style that you recognize or maybe it looks like you have stepped back in time?

7. Notice too if you are alone. Your ancestor could already be in the room waiting for you, or maybe they enter after you. You could sense their presence and hear their voice or receive a vision.

8. Take your time and let your ancestor speak through your intuition. Relax and enjoy the experience. Don't feel you have to force anything. If nothing happens, that's fine. You are totally in control of this visualization, and you can leave at any time.

9. If you do meet your ancestor, you may want to ask them for a specific message or piece of advice, or you might prefer simply to let the conversation go where it needs to. They may want to send you healing energy or just sit with you. Remember that they too will have questions. This is a conversation and a way of getting to know each other better.

10. When you're ready to return to your physical body, take a minute to thank your ancestor for their time and guidance, then say goodbye. Know that you can come here again, whenever you need to reconnect.

11. Walk back through the door, along the corridor, and up the winding staircase. Count out your steps as you did on the way down until you reach the top.

12. Take a deep breath in and, as you exhale, open your eyes. You might want to give your body a shake or take a couple of sips of water to center yourself.

13. Have your journal handy and write down anything you can remember from the experience. You can chart your progress each time you perform this visualization, and over time you'll notice how your relationship with your ancestor develops. Remember that you can visit any of the rooms along the corridor and meet different ancestors at any time.

Meditation

Meditation helps to calm and still the mind, allowing your intuition to rise to the surface. It opens a window in your mind and soul, which lets your ancestors send their healing and wisdom. It's a powerful tool that combines breathing techniques with other tips and tricks to silence thoughts and bring you into the present moment. It can also help you reach higher states of consciousness, from which you can commune with your ancestral guides in the spirit world.

TRY THIS!

Flower of Light

1. Find a quiet spot where you can sit undisturbed. Relax your body and close your eyes.
2. Take a long, deep breath in through your nose. Hold for five counts, then release gently through your mouth.
3. Continue to breathe in this way for a few minutes. If you find your concentration slipping, don't worry. Bring your attention back to each breath and the counting process.
4. As you continue to breathe, bring your focus to the middle of your scalp. Feel a bristling sensation, as the energy center here begins to open up. If it helps, imagine a golden flower bud slowly unfurling its petals until it is fully in bloom.
5. In the center of the flower is a whirling golden ball of energy that is connected to your higher self. This is a direct conduit to your intuition and the spiritual realm.
6. As you draw in each breath, imagine this ball of energy getting bigger and brighter. See the light it emits extending outward in every direction.

"The language of love flows between me and my ancestors."

7. As you exhale, imagine releasing any fear and doubt. Let go of all the negative energy and stress that you have been holding onto.

8. Continue to breathe in this way, focusing on the golden ball of energy.

9. If any thoughts come to you during this time, acknowledge their existence, then file them away. Bring your attention back to the pattern of your breath.

10. You might feel emotions rise to the surface or even hear voices. Be aware of them. Let them flow through your mind as you continue to focus on your breathing.

11. When you are ready, visualize the golden flower gradually closing its petals and bring your attention back to the rise and fall of your chest and the rest of your body.

12. How do you feel in this moment? Check in with yourself and notice any changes in your mood.

13. Slowly open your eyes and give your limbs a stretch. Take your time coming back to the real world.

14. If you received a vision or any insight while meditating, be sure to note this down in your journal. Keep a record of anything you can remember for future reference. Remember, this is one of the many ways your ancestors will reach out to you.

"My ancestral guides are with me at all times."

Practical Psychic Activities

There are practical ways you can communicate with your ancestors, which might appeal if you struggle with techniques like visualization and meditation. Like those who went before you, we are all different. Some of us find it easy to think visually and picture a scenario, or quieten our mind with a breathing exercise, while others prefer to be more active and send a message using other methods. Your ancestors want to share their wisdom and communicate with you. They want to help and send their love, just as you want to make that connection with them. It's important to do what feels comfortable for you, so if you're more practically minded, then you might want to communicate through writing, speaking, performing a ritual, or working with a specific memory.

TRY THIS!

A Letter to the Past

One of the simplest ways to connect with your ancestors is to write down what you want to say. A letter that captures how you feel, what you'd like to know, and what you would say to them if you were face-to-face is a great starting point.

YOU WILL NEED

Photograph of your ancestor, rough paper, writing paper, pen, envelope, journal

1. Start by identifying an ancestor who you would like to speak with. For example, you could choose one of your great-grandparents. It doesn't matter if you don't know much about them, as this is about making a spiritual connection.

2. If you have any photographs of the ancestor you have chosen, place them on a table in front of you.

3. Imagine that you are meeting this person for the first time. What would you like to say to them and what would you like them to know about you? Remember this is a two-way process, so while you'll have questions for them, they will also want to learn about you and your life.

4. Write a few notes on rough paper to start with to help you craft your letter, then when you're ready, take a sheet of writing paper and begin.

5. Introduce yourself, as you would if you were meeting them in the flesh. Ask them about their life and tell them about your own. If you have any recollections or memories of them, share these, and mention the people in your family who also remember them.

6. Thank your ancestor for their presence in your life and for their guidance, and if you have any specific questions or you need help with anything, ask them. This is your chance to put it all down on paper.

7. When you're happy with your letter, read it aloud. Imagine they're standing there beside you, listening to what you have to say.

8. To finish, seal the letter in an envelope and address it to your ancestor. You can either keep this in your journal or place it on your ancestral altar (see page 82).

Automatic Writing

Automatic writing can help you tap into inner wisdom and connect with the spiritual realm. Some people believe that it helps them commune with their guides in the afterlife, while for others it's a way of tuning into the subconscious mind, which provides a channel to those in spirit.

As with many psychic practices, you'll need to keep an open heart and mind, and be prepared to practice this skill, but it is well worth the effort because it will help you communicate with your ancestors at a deeper level. The key is to enter a trance-like state by relaxing your mind. This can be done by using various breathing techniques, playing soothing music, or simply sitting in nature. Once you feel calm, you are ready to relinquish control, put pen to paper, and let your ancestors speak through you.

TRY THIS!
Conversations in Nature

1. To begin, find a comfortable spot where you can sit in nature. This could be in your backyard or a local park or beauty spot. Take your journal and a pen with you.
2. Make sure you are comfortable and in a place where you won't be disturbed. It's important not to put a time limit on this exercise and to give yourself the freedom to relax.
3. Take a couple of long, deep breaths to calm your mind. Connect with the environment by engaging each of your senses. This will help you to be still in the moment.
4. Close your eyes for a couple of minutes and focus on your connection with your ancestors. You might want to ask them to make themselves known to you, or to be with you as you sit.
5. Rather than concentrating on a specific question, leave the parameters open. Invite them in and let them speak through you, but give them the freedom to say anything they want. If they want to give you a message, they will.
6. Hold the pen over the paper and don't think about what it is doing. If it helps, keep your eyes closed or look away.
7. If you find yourself controlling what is written, stop and bring your focus back to your breathing.

> "I am protected, supported, and loved by those who went before."

8. Take your time and have breaks when you feel it's necessary. Most importantly, do not worry if you don't get anything, or if what you have written seems like gibberish. This is perfectly natural.

9. When you're ready, pause for a moment to shake out your limbs and take a couple of deep breaths to center yourself, then have a look at what you have written.

10. You may see patterns in the writing or key words that stand out and mean something. Sometimes parts of a phrase will emerge from the text. Highlight anything that sticks out or seems significant.

11. As you continue to practice this psychic skill, you may notice a recurring message or repeated words coming through. You'll begin to develop a way of writing that you understand and the messages you receive from your ancestors will start to make sense.

12. Over time, you'll have more detailed conversations with your ancestors, and automatic writing will become an easy way for you to communicate.

Scrying

This is a form of divination, where you gaze upon a reflective surface to focus your mind. As you become more relaxed, your psychic senses take over and you may see patterns or images. You may even experience a vision. Sometimes the insight comes in the form of a feeling or just "knowing" something. Scrying can be a useful tool when you're trying to communicate with your ancestors. It's another pathway that they can use to send you a message.

TRY THIS!

Mirror Meditation

Most scrying mirrors are black and often made from obsidian, so as not to reflect any kind of image. This gives the mind free rein, so the subconscious can "see" and "read" any signs from the spirit world. For this exercise, you will use a normal mirror to provide focus and clarity.

1. Sit in front of the mirror and let your gaze fall upon its surface. Don't stare or strain, just relax your focus and breathe deeply.
2. In your mind or out loud, ask that your ancestors draw close with loving energy. You might want to request a sign or message, or simply let them guide you in their own way.
3. Let your mind drift and continue to soften your gaze.
4. Patterns may emerge in the mirror, or you might just get a feeling or sudden burst of inspiration. Let any thoughts or messages flow through your mind. Don't try to pin them down, just let them rise and fall away.
5. Notice any dominant emotions and let them flow through you.
6. Don't worry if nothing happens at first. This skill takes patience and practice, but it is well worth the effort, as it's something you can do quickly and easily when you need guidance or to feel protected and supported by your ancestors.

Memory Work

While you won't recollect your distant ancestors, you may well have memories of your immediate family, like your grandparents and your great-grandparents, and you will be able to connect with them through these shared moments. All you need to do is bring the memory to mind and relive the experience. While it's highly unlikely that you'll recall every detail, you will remember the emotions associated with the memory, so this is a good place to start.

TRY THIS!
Mindful Memories

1. Set some time aside and create a relaxing atmosphere, so you can explore each memory at your leisure.
2. Close your eyes and recreate the memory in your mind. Take in as much detail as you can and engage all your senses, considering not only what you can see, but also what you can hear, smell, touch, and feel.
3. Immerse yourself in the moment by reliving the emotions associated with the memory.
4. Let the memory play out in your mind several times and enjoy the experience of reconnecting with your ancestors.
5. To finish, you might want to say an affirmation, something along the lines of: "As I recollect this moment, I open the channels of communication with my ancestor and strengthen the bonds between us."

You can take this exercise a step further once you have been through the memory a few times and you're more familiar with it. Get to a point in the memory where you feel happy pausing it and freezing the frame, just as you would a movie or the TV. Take a moment to breathe and then formulate a question or something you'd like to know in your mind, or, if you prefer, just ask for guidance or an insight that will help you in the future. Yes, you will be deviating from the script of your memory, but that's okay. This is your memory,

and you are allowed to use it as a gateway to connect with your ancestor and ask for guidance.

Do not worry if you don't get anything back when you first do this exercise. Just relax and let the memory play out. Sometimes the guidance will come at another time, perhaps in a dream or a sudden burst of inspiration. It may be that you are guided in another way—perhaps you receive healing or a wave of comfort at a time when you feel vulnerable. You might suddenly feel stronger and more focused in your aims or find that you implicitly "know" what you need to do, as if the answer has been with you all along. Your ancestors will speak to you in lots of different ways, so it's about being open to the spiritual realm and trusting your intuition.

"Ancestral wisdom lives within me."

Dream Interventions

When you sleep, your conscious mind takes a step back and allows your subconscious to take control, and it is through this that your intuition speaks to you. The messages you receive in dreams are often potent and insightful, making this the ideal medium for you not only to communicate with your ancestors, but also to receive healing and guidance.

Sleep on it Ritual

1. Sit on the edge of the bed and take a couple of long, deep breaths to calm your mind.
2. Hold a piece of amethyst in both hands. This beautiful stone stimulates your Third Eye chakra, which is linked to your intuition. It also helps you to communicate with the spiritual realm.
3. Close your eyes and bring to mind any issues you may have. If you're seeking healing, then open your heart and ask for it. Address your ancestors as if they were in the room with you, saying, "I am open and ready to receive your guidance. I ask for your help and healing when dealing with this issue. Guide me and inspire me."
4. Place the amethyst beneath your pillow and keep a notebook and pen by your bed.
5. Say, "I release my worries. I open myself up to you, my ancestors, and trust that you will come to my aid."
6. Continue to breathe deeply, focusing on the gentle rhythm and the rise and fall of your chest. Let go of any fear or anxiety, and trust that you will receive the help you need while you sleep.
7. On waking, make a note of any dreams you had. Even if they don't make sense, the imagery and symbolism within them could prove insightful in the future.

8. Don't worry if you can't recall your dreams. Repeat the process for the next few nights and make a note of how you feel each morning. Notice any changes in your mood, outlook, and energy levels.

9. Be assured that your ancestors are dealing with it. They hold you in their hearts and will deliver the healing and guidance you need, whether it's in the form of a dream or sending healing energy while you sleep.

YOU WILL NEED

Amethyst crystal, notebook, pen

Journal Exercise

Reflect upon what you have discovered so far about your ancestors and the different ways that you can converse with them. Do you feel the connection between you? Have you found a way of communicating that works for you, and how does this make you feel? Is there anything you can do to improve the flow of communication? Consider any signs or messages that you have received so far. Do you feel this has made a difference to your life, and if so, how?

What would you like to talk about with your ancestors? Make a list of subjects and areas where you could benefit from their wisdom.

Consider how you feel now you know that you're not alone, that your ancestors surround you and send you their love and guidance. Write down key words to sum up your emotions and use these to create positive affirmations, such as "I am safe. I am loved. I am not alone."

What's Your Family Story?

This chapter looks at the tales that have been passed down through the generations within your family—from the stories that you tell yourself, and how these influence your life, to those memory tales that form repeated narratives in your mind. Then there are the stories that have become a part of your family folklore, the recognized tales that have evolved over time and taken on new life. You will learn how to uncover the deeper meaning and themes that arise from these narratives, as well as how to identify the core message within them and change this to create a positive outlook and future.

"The story of my ancestors is in my blood."

The Oral Tradition

Stories enable us to make sense of the world. They help us understand why things work the way they do. Sometimes we make the stories up to explain a phenomenon or happening in nature that we don't fully comprehend. Sometimes the stories are more personal to us. They help us build a common landscape between family, friends, and the wider community. There's a long tradition of storytelling in cultures from around the world. It was how we learned and evolved: by listening to the stories of our ancestors. We heard about their exploits, the things they did that worked and the things that didn't. We grew in strength and confidence and became inspired by these tales. They helped to shape us, to create a belief system that we could follow together. Most importantly, these narratives helped us bond and connect with each other.

The oral tradition was a way of retaining history, of charting our progress in life, and it is still relevant today. You may think that the digital age relies heavily on technology, but we are still telling stories. Social media platforms such as Twitter, Facebook, and Instagram reveal what we have been up to, telling tales of everyday reality and the things that matter to us. Social media is a way of creating a narrative about yourself that others can see and react to. Voice notes are a method of communication for delivering stories that our friends and families can pick up at any time. The tech may have advanced, but we are still sharing stories and using them to make sense of the world and our place within it.

With the past in mind and knowing the power of your ancestral connections, it's even more important to consider the tales that have been passed down your family line. Some of these stories will be personal, based on memories of real events. Some will be made up or adapted, used as a teaching tool and a way of passing on information. Some will be more subtle, narratives that have slipped into the subconscious over time and now influence the way you think and feel. You will also encounter tales that have spread, come from the wider community, and been shaped by the way your ancestors lived. It's up to you to decipher these tales and their meaning for you right now, to sift through the stories and find their core truth. In doing so, you will also discover the power of storytelling and how you can use it to manifest your reality. You'll uncover your own personal tales—the ones you carry in your heart—and learn how they guide and motivate you.

What's Your Narrative?

You might not think you have a narrative, but there will be more than one story that runs through your family grouping. Thousands of tales feature in your life, from the stories you tell yourself to the memory tales that you repeat in your mind and share with others. Then there are those gems of family folklore that have been regaled many times. Stories come in all shapes and sizes, but it's the effect they have on you that really counts. The tales you encounter have the power to shape you, to shift your perspective, and even to teach you something.

"Narratives are the gift that keep on giving."

Family Folk Tales

Folk tales are cultural. These are the stories that are passed down, the urban legends and tales that might not fully make sense. Sometimes otherworldly, sometimes based on fact, they are the narratives we love and learn to live by—the stories that have become a part of our community. From myths and legends to superstitions and old wives' tales, they play an important role in our culture and reveal how the people of the past thought and acted.

Family folk tales serve the same purpose. These are the stories you know and cherish. Like treasured heirlooms, they're the tales that have become folklore, the ones that are regaled at every gathering or celebration. Stories like that of old Uncle Gilbert and his magic pipe—one puff was all it took to make a wish come true—or the time Great Aunt Hettie faced off a pack of wild dogs. They might be exaggerated for entertainment value (something everyone is aware of), but there's an element of truth to them. So maybe it was just one dog that Hettie took on, rather than a pack, but the fact remains that she showed incredible courage in the narrative.

If you were to pull these tales apart and consider what really happened, it might take some of the magic away, so instead you suspend judgment and enjoy each story for what it is. Even so, family folk tales tell you a lot about your family and what drives it. There is a reason why these narratives stand the test of time and why they're kept alive and told over and again. Perhaps it's because they uphold certain values and beliefs that were, and still are, important to your family? Maybe there's a lesson or guidance hidden within the tale, or it could be that the spirit of the story says something about your family as a whole. To gain a deeper insight, all you have to do is ask some questions:

- Who is at the heart of the tale?
- What do you know about this family member?
- What does the story tell you about this family member?
- Is the ending positive or negative?
- What can you learn from the tale?
- How do you feel when you hear/share the story?

The answers to these questions will help you peel away the layers, so you can understand the key themes, messages, and any beliefs that are contained within the narrative.

Memory Tales

These tales are the most potent type of narrative because they're based on personal experience. They resonate deeply with our psyche, and if replayed constantly can actually program the way we think, feel, and act.

Working with Memory Tales

We all have good and bad memories that we can draw upon. Sometimes these recollections work in our favor, reminding us of cherished moments and times when we achieved something of value. Reliving these narratives can help us feel joyful and positive about the future. They can imbue us with confidence in our abilities. Negative memories are equally powerful. If replayed often enough, they can make us fearful and insecure. Occasionally, something will happen that triggers the narrative, and once more you find yourself back in a memory, recalling every detail. As you continue to relive the memory, it reprograms the way you think and what you believe about yourself, which can have a negative effect on you.

It's important to consider perspective when working with memory tales. How you remember something may be very different to how another member of your family recalls the situation. As you explore the world of family storytelling and discover the ancestral tales that have been passed down, you'll realize that perspective plays an important role in the retelling of the narrative and can be easily tweaked to help you regain control and switch the theme to something more positive.

TRY THIS!
Picture It

This exercise is a creative way to work with memory tales. You can do it on your own, but it's also fun to practice with family members. It helps the conversation flow, and you may hear some stories that you've never heard before, which in turn will help you connect with your nearest and dearest at a deeper level.

1. To begin, think of a memory. This could be a memory from childhood or something more recent. You could even pick something that has happened to you earlier in the week. This is an introduction to working with narratives, so it's about getting used to sharing stories and looking at the themes and the core message within.

2. Choose a memory that is positive, so for example you might recall a time when you achieved a goal, such as passing your driving test or an exam, climbing a mountain, and so on. You could also pick a happy event, perhaps a birthday, wedding, or a particularly memorable vacation.

3. Once you have a memory in mind, run through it once more. Relive the experience and all of the emotions. When you get to a point in the story that sums up what the memory is all about, freeze the frame. Imagine you have paused the narrative at this point. So, if you were climbing a mountain for charity, you might freeze the frame when you reach the pinnacle and you've achieved your aim.

4. Take the picture you have in your mind and try drawing it on a piece of paper. You don't have to be the best artist in the world, as this is just about getting an image down that represents the memory. So, if you prefer, you can draw something more symbolic. You can be as creative as you like at this point and enjoy the process of recreating that moment on the paper.

5. When you've finished, turn the paper over and write "This is a story about..." and fill in the blank space. You only have a sentence, so be brief and summarize the tale.

6. Now challenge yourself to think of a key word that sums up what the memory is all about for you. This can be difficult. Our natural instinct is to explain in detail, so be strict with yourself. The word could be an emotion like "joy" or "excitement." It could relate to the situation, so it might be "adventure" or "freedom." It's entirely up to you which word you pick. This is the core message of the narrative.

7. If you're working with other family members, you might want to swap pictures at this point and ask them to tell you what they think the story is about, without looking at what you have written. This can be a fun way of sharing tales and learning about each other. Once they've had a go at saying what they think the memory is about, you can let them read what you have written and go on to tell the tale in more detail.

8. Once you have created your picture and identified the core message behind the narrative, you will be able to work with it and even change the message in order to manifest a positive outcome.

YOU WILL NEED

Lots of paper, some pens and pencils

Change Your Story

It's possible to take a memory and shift the focus from negative to positive, with a little creative effort and your imagination. In doing so, you'll regain control and take back the power.

TRY THIS!

Switch Your Storyboard

1. For this exercise, choose a different memory to the one you worked with in Picture It, something that is not as positive. For example, a memory of a meeting at work that didn't go so well or a presentation where you feel you could have done better.
2. You are going to use this memory to create a storyboard, so take a sheet of paper and draw a series of squares like a comic strip along the center. Each square is going to tell a stage of the story in picture form. Again, if you prefer, you can use symbols to represent what happens.
3. Beneath each drawing you're going to write a sentence to describe what is happening in that square—in effect, you're telling the story using a few words and images. Keep this simple. It doesn't need to be wordy; you are only telling the essence of the tale.
4. Now think of a word to sum up the memory, as you did for the previous exercise.
5. Read through the boxes and when you reach the last one, bring to mind the core message that you have identified as being at the heart of this narrative. This is what you want to re-enforce with your ending. So, if at the end of the memory you felt that something didn't go well, show this through your expression or a symbol to represent that feeling.
6. Now look at your story again and consider the core message. If you could change this message to something more positive, what word would you use? For example, if your tale left you feeling fearful, then you might swap "fear" for "courage" or "confidence."
7. Write your new core message on the back of the paper.

8. Now you're going to tell the story again with this core message in mind, so use the same boxes to begin the tale, but when you reach the point of crisis in the story—the point at which your story could go in any direction—create a series of new boxes with different pictures inside to reflect your new core message.

9. You can come up with as many alternative endings as you'd like until you're happy with how the story ends. The important thing is that the ending reflects your new, more positive core message.

10. Read through your new version of the memory several times. Repeat the narrative out loud and relive it in your mind, but with the alternative ending. Embrace your senses and really feel each emotion as you do this, to make the memory as real as possible.

11. To finish, take your new core message and work it into an affirmation that you can repeat throughout the day. For example, if you changed your core message from "fear" to "courage," then you might say, "I am filled with courage and strength."

12. Set some time aside every day to go through the story at least once and do this with as much feeling as you can.

YOU WILL NEED

Lots of paper, some pens and pencils

Ancestral Memories and Tales

Once you have tried the last exercise with one of your own memories, you can do exactly the same thing with tales that have been passed down through the generations. This works particularly well if the tale has a negative resolution. For example, you may have heard that your great-grandfather lived in poverty for most of his life. This is not necessarily something you would feel happy about, and it could potentially affect your own view of money and how you manage your finances. It's easy to assume that anyone hearing this story would focus on the negative aspects and how difficult life must have been for their ancestor. You can switch this up by retelling the tale in a positive way. While you can't change history, you can bring out the positive themes associated with this narrative.

TRY THIS!
A Day in the Life

1. Take a sheet of paper and write a paragraph describing your ancestor's daily life. You don't have to know their entire life story to do this, just imagine what a day would be like for them. So you might start with them waking up and describe their surroundings, and then talk about their struggles throughout the day.
2. Also consider the people your ancestor shared their life with and what impact this had on them.
3. Once you have completed your short narrative, read it back and think about the key themes that arise from what you have written. For example, you might feel a sense of desperation or frustration at the situation, and that your ancestor felt powerless.
4. Now write down a handful of words that you associate with the themes, so you might choose "desperation," "fear," and "anger."
5. Next replace these words with positive alternatives. For instance, you might swap "desperation" for "hope," "fear" for "self-reliance," and "anger" for "drive."
6. You now have three very different themes to work with, and they are still relevant to your tale.
7. Go back through the narrative and rework it by weaving in a sense of "hope." Consider how you ancestor would have awoken each day, feeling hopeful and ready for the challenges ahead. Think about the "self-reliance" they must have had to survive at that time and also the innate "drive" that pushed them onward.

8. Rewrite the paragraph with these new themes in mind and read it aloud.
9. While you haven't changed the story, you are now able to look at it from a different, more positive perspective. You're acknowledging the difficulties, but also looking for the gifts hidden within. This will help you develop a more positive mindset in your own life.

YOU WILL NEED

A sheet of paper and a pen

"I am the author of my own tale."

Ancestral Memory Tales

These tales from the past are the same as your own memories. They are based on personal recollections that have been retold over the centuries and passed from one family grouping to another. Over time, the stories will have evolved and key elements may have changed. It's important to be aware that the tale you hear today could be very different from the original, but that doesn't matter. The essential truth will still be there, and you will be able to learn a lot about your ancestors and strengthen your connection with them. Any family story is a treasure, as it provides an opportunity to explore your heritage and draw strength and power from the bonds you share. Here are some key tips on how you can make the most of those family narratives.

Put Yourself in the Story

When we hear stories about other people, whether they're related to us or fictional characters, we become connected to them, particularly if we can identify with some aspects of their personality or situation. Writers know this, which is why they create characters and scenarios that you can relate to. In effect, they place you in the story and devise it so you can imagine being there and experiencing the same things. You can do the same with oral stories by putting yourself in the tale. Imagine you are your ancestor. You are the main protagonist. Put yourself at the center of the action and imagine how you might feel and what you would do.

Top Tip

It can be helpful to write the tale from a first-person point of view, so you become your ancestor and retell what happened by engaging your emotions and senses.

Record the Narratives

Reading a story is one thing, but hearing a tale is an entirely different experience. Certain nuances of emotion only come through when we hear someone speak and bring the words to life. If you can, get recordings of the tales that are important to your family. You can do this by recording family members as they share a tale with you, or you can create your own version and record yourself reading it aloud. Doing this is also a good way to help you identify with the narrative and the underlying message.

Top Tip

Plan out your tale by splitting it into sections, so you would have a paragraph for the beginning where you set the scene and context, a paragraph for the middle where the action tends to take place, and one for the ending where you bring everything to a satisfactory conclusion. Once you have this story plan, practice reading it aloud before you record it. Pretend you're onstage delivering a performance. You'll get more out of the story, and it will sound better too.

"The stories of my ancestors sing to my soul."

Celebrate the Tales

There is a gift in every story. Even the darkest of tales holds a kernel of truth or a lesson that is worth remembering. Cautionary tales guide and advise us, stories that pull at the heart strings develop empathy, and uplifting tales provide strength and encouragement when times are tough. It's important to celebrate every story you hear and to find something of worth within the tale. Say "thank you for this gift" as you commit the story to memory or reflect upon it. Share the tale if you feel it will help others and work with it to uncover the deeper meaning.

Top Tip

Read a variety of different types of stories and get used to discovering the truth in each one. This will help you understand that narratives have many layers, and the same goes for those stories that are important to your family.

Create a Family Memoir

Once you have collected a number of stories, you might want to catalog them and create a memoir, which should include all of the tales in a similar format. By organizing them in this way, you'll be able to see the types of story that are most popular within your family group, as well as the recurring themes and messages. It's up to you how you arrange the stories. You could group together all the tales from a specific era or about a certain person, or you could do this by theme. Having the stories all together in one place provides a resource, which you can dip into when you need guidance or want to feel close to your ancestors.

Top Tip

Leave some space to add your own entries. Remember, family stories are a living, breathing record of your life and will continue to be passed down through the generations. When you put together your own tales, be sure to consider any lessons, guidance, or messages that you'd like future family members to understand.

Create Your Own Story Ritual

Each time you unearth a story, mark the moment by performing a simple ritual to evoke the power of the tale. This could be something like lighting a candle and retelling the tale, or thinking about the key themes and what they mean to you. You could say a few words or add an entry to your journal that relates to the story.

Top Tip

Try to incorporate this ritual into your routine by creating a regular slot for it in your schedule. For example, you might choose the end of the week to sit and reflect upon the stories you've gathered, or a particular evening to write about them in your journal.

Start a Storytelling Circle

Gathering family stories can be fun and a way of getting to know your relatives better. Storytelling is a communal thing, and it brings people together, so why not use it as an excuse to throw a party or get some of your nearest and dearest together for a story-sharing session. A storytelling circle might sound formal, but it's a relaxed way of sharing tales, sitting in a group around a fire/fireplace, and taking the opportunity to tell a story from the past. How you tell a story is up to you. Some people prefer to be asked questions as prompts, while others will naturally enjoy the process of telling the story.

Top Tip

You can ask people to bring an item related to the tale and place it in the center of the circle. T his works particularly well if you have family heirlooms. You can then pick an object and the teller will use this as a starting point to deliver the tale. This kind of circle is a lovely way of getting to know more about your family and your ancestors, while enjoying their company at the same time.

Acknowledge Word Power

The tales we tell ourselves are the most powerful, and we do this all the time. You only have to listen to snippets of conversation to hear people exchanging stories. More importantly, if you listen to your thoughts, you will hear certain narratives repeated. Meditation will help you quieten your mind and become more aware of this internal chatter. The next step is to ask yourself whether the narratives you repeat are true, and if you are using positive or negative language. We often find it easier to focus on our faults and the things we have done wrong. We replay emotions and use words that we wouldn't use with anyone else. For example, if you find yourself constantly saying "I can't do this, I am useless/rubbish/dreadful" and then spiral into stories of when you have fallen short in some way, you are re-enforcing the idea in your mind and using words in a negative way.

Top Tip

The next time you find yourself repeating a negative narrative in your mind, say "STOP" loudly in your head. Switch the thought and replace it with something positive. Be aware of the power of words and how you use them with yourself and others.

"Words empower me and bring me closer to my family, past and present."

Journal Exercise

Take a moment to consider all the stories you have heard, shared, and remembered while doing the exercises in this chapter. How do they make you feel? Perhaps you now have a greater understanding of certain family members or feel more connected to the past after exploring each tale? Reflect on the emotional journey you have taken and consider which particular stories stand out for you. Why is this? Some narratives will resonate because you have been through, or are going through, similar things in your own life, and some will strike a chord because you identify with the main protagonist. Some stories will offer advice, while others might instill hope, confidence, or strength. Consider the gifts of each tale.

Now think about the stories you tell yourself and others. Are there any tales that you find yourself repeating often? Do certain words or narratives pop up again and again. Why is this? Consider if these are positive or negative in influence and how you might work with them to change the way you think and feel.

Finally, think of a story that you'd like to leave behind for your ancestors. You might already have a tale in mind or you may want to make one up about yourself and your life. List any ideas as bullet points that you can come back to or use when you're in a creative mood.

_____

_____

_____

_____

_____

_____

_____

_____

_____

_____

_____

_____

_____

"The stories I tell myself shape my reality."

CHAPTER
FOUR

Ancestral Karma and How to Work With It

This chapter looks at the ancestral karma that you carry with you, and how to heal it. Karma can be positive or negative, so learning about ancestral karma is one way you can connect with your ancestors at a deeper level and truly understand their motivations and the struggles they faced. The sense of healing this brings will help you feel empowered and free from restriction. It will also strengthen your ancestral bonds and create a sense of belonging, as you become more aware of what makes you tick, and why.

"The dreams of my ancestors flow through my veins."

What Is Karma?

To work with ancestral karma, you must first understand the role of karma in your life and what it means for you. Karma comes from the Sanskrit word for action, and it is this that is at the root of everything. Our thoughts influence our actions, which in turn help to create our reality. While it's easy to believe the old adage of "what goes around, comes around," and that karma is the Universe's way of dishing out some kind of judgment, in reality it is about you, how you feel, and how you perceive things.

For example, if you try to see the positive in everything, then you're more likely to be in a good mood. This means others will relate to you positively and your interactions will go well. If you walk around feeling miserable and believing the world is full of doom and gloom, then you will tend to focus on the bad things. Your mood will be affected, and so your interactions are likely to be on the negative side. If you're in a negative frame of mind and meet someone who is the opposite and radiating joy, then this may affect your own viewpoint. In effect, their positive thoughts, which translate into positive actions, are a catalyst to bring about a positive change in you. This is karma at work. Ultimately, it's an energy exchange between yourself and the wider world. What we think and believe to be true influences what we do and our daily experience, and it has the power to affect not only our own reality, but also that of the people with whom we come into contact. It's an ongoing cycle and something we must keep working on.

Good Karma

Get into a good karma mindset by paying attention to the way you interact with yourself and the world around you.

TRY THIS!

Connect with the Positive

Do this exercise to help you stay in a positive mindset and create good karma.

1. The next time you're in a good mood, pay attention. Notice little things like your posture: how you stand and hold yourself. How you walk and talk. Perhaps you feel taller, or there's a bounce in your step, or maybe you are more open and relaxed, which in turn allows you to breathe more deeply.
2. Notice the thoughts going around in your head and the kind, encouraging words that you use with yourself and others.
3. Pay attention to the way you interact with the world—perhaps you engage your senses more to connect with your surroundings.
4. All these things are a result of how you feel, but it's a two-way process. You can also change your mood by doing these things. This means that when you're feeling low or pessimistic, you can check in with your posture and ensure you're standing tall. You can look at your breathing and take longer, deeper breaths, so your body is fueled with oxygen. You can listen to your thoughts and swap negative ones for those that are more positive, and you can engage with the world by using your senses and living in the moment.
5. If you get into the habit of following through with simple checks and paying attention to yourself and your mood, over time you will reprogram your mind to think differently and create good karma.

What Is Ancestral Karma?

Ancestral karma is all about the habits, behaviors, and beliefs that you have inherited from your ancestors. These are often carried down through the generations subconsciously. Just like regular karma, it relies on the pattern of cause and effect.

For example, you might think you'll never be able to save any money because your parents and grandparents found it hard to put money aside. Each day was a struggle to make ends meet and because you have seen and experienced this way of operating, you now believe the same thing about your own life. So you scrimp and count the pennies, focusing on what you don't have rather than what you do. Your attitude and approach have been formed by what you have witnessed, but it is just your perception and not the reality. This is inherited karma. You have accepted that this is the way it will be, based on what you know to be true from your family. The good news is you can break the cycle and change this, with a little work.

If you do some digging into your family history, you will probably discover that this karma goes back many generations. Life was most likely hard for your ancestors, and they survived day by day through sheer hard work and determination. But the cycle continues as each family grouping copies the beliefs and habits of the previous one. Even though you have inherited this way of thinking, there is much to be admired here.

Once you start looking at the past and considering how things were for your ancestors, you realize how these ideas were formed. You see the strength and resilience that have also passed along your family line, and you can recognize these traits in yourself. Ancestral karma doesn't have to be negative. It's a tool for self-reflection, and once you start delving into the patterns and behaviors you have inherited, you'll learn more about yourself, your family, and your roots, which in turn will help you feel more empowered.

Common Inherited Beliefs

To help you identify ancestral karma, here is a list of common beliefs that are often passed down the family line:

- Fear of change
- Fear of a specific thing, such as dogs or thunder and lightning
- Fear of authority
- Fear of something that is different
- Fear of being loved or loving yourself
- Fear of abandonment
- Fear of not having enough
- Thinking you are not good enough
- Worrying about the future
- Believing that you are not worthy of reward
- Believing that life must always be a struggle
- Believing that others are untrustworthy
- Believing that you are always at fault
- Believing that you cannot survive without something, whether this is a person or a habit
- Believing that you have an addictive personality
- Believing that the only way others will like you is if you conform to their beliefs and opinions
- Believing you cannot do something (that is, a specific skill)

TRY THIS!
Reflect and Reprogram

1. Take your journal and spend a little time thinking about your experience of family life. Consider the qualities that you admire about those closest to you. Think also about the beliefs you share with your nearest and dearest and the habits you have inherited. Do any stand out? Perhaps you and your siblings share a competitive streak, or prefer to avoid confrontation and have learned to bottle up your feelings.

2. Take each habit/behavior and write a sentence that sums it up, then spend some time pondering where it came from. What is at the root of this behavior? For example, if you struggle to save money, this may come from a belief that you don't have enough and never will. Lack is at the heart of this karma, and there's an inherent need for security.

3. Once you have identified the core root of the karma, consider how you can take steps to change it. For example, if you struggle with a fear of never having enough, think of ways you can make yourself feel more secure. You might acknowledge all the things and people that make your life richer. This will help you realize that you do have plenty and should enable you to eliminate the sense of "lack" you feel.

4. Let your thoughts flow, and if any ideas come to you, note them down. Don't worry if nothing springs to mind. This is about self-reflection and ascertaining what your ancestral karma might be. The more open you become to this, the more ideas and answers will present themselves in time.

5. Make a point of doing this exercise once a month, taking each belief or behavior and giving yourself time to reflect upon it and consider the steps you can take to bring about positive change.

"I work hard to break the patterns of the past and create new, positive habits."

TRY THIS!
Ancestral Altar

One of the most effective ways to honor your ancestors and work with their karma is to create an ancestral altar in your home. This doesn't have to be elaborate, just think of it as a simple way to pay homage to your ancestors. It's a place where you can spend time and connect with them. You'll be able to use the altar when you're working with ancestral karma and when you're looking for spiritual guidance from your ancestors.

YOU WILL NEED

Sage oil in an oil burner (or a bundle of dried sage), personal items, crystals, flowers, candle

1. Start by creating the space. This can be the corner of a room, a small coffee table, a shelf, or a windowsill.
2. Choose a space that is easily accessible and clear it in preparation. You might want to burn some sage oil in an oil burner, or light a bundle of dried sage to cleanse the area of negative vibrations.
3. Next decorate the altar with items that mean something to you, your family, and your ancestors. Old photographs, pictures, and mementoes of time spent together will help you connect with lost loved ones, as will family heirlooms.
4. Crystals like amethyst and quartz will help to amplify energy and connect you to the spiritual realm, while also boosting psychic powers.
5. Flowers are a lovely addition too, as they represent new growth, and they are also a way to honor your ancestors.
6. Finally, place a candle on your altar. You will be able to use this in rituals when you wish to reflect or connect with your ancestral guides.

TRY THIS!
Altar Ritual to Release Ancestral Karma

1. Set aside some time when you won't be disturbed, so you can relax and be in the moment.
2. Light the candle on your ancestral altar and gaze into the flame. This will help you clear your mind. Breathe deeply and let your thoughts settle.
3. Take your time and look at the photographs you have placed on the altar—the family members, past and present, who have influenced your life. Think about each one, and as you do, give thanks for that person. Even if you never met them, or know little about them, it doesn't matter. This is about acknowledging their presence and the role they have played in shaping who you are today.
4. Imagine that these family members are there with you, sharing this moment of reflection. Say, "I am honored to have you by my side."
5. Place both hands over your heart, take a deep breath in, and, as you release that breath, say a few words to express gratitude for your ancestors. Thank them for looking out for you, for their spiritual guidance, and for the gifts and talents that you have inherited from them.
6. Finally, address your family karma by acknowledging those habits and behaviors that you have inherited and express your forgiveness. Even if you are unsure about your karma, say, "I understand that this was not intentional, and that I have inherited this karma from my ancestors. I am ready to acknowledge and release this, so that I can move forward and step into my power."
7. Take a deep breath in and, as you exhale, blow out the candle.
8. Sit quietly and reflect upon the exercise. You may want to make a few notes in your journal about how you're feeling, or simply enjoy this peaceful moment of healing.

Heal Your Karma

When we form beliefs, particularly those that have been influenced by others, we give them energy. We bring them to life in our hearts and minds, and they become bonds that tie us in place. This can be a good thing because it helps us feel secure and rooted, but if the karma has a negative impact, then the ties become chains and we become trapped. Each time we do something to affirm that belief, good or bad, the bonds become tighter. They fix us to the spot, and it becomes harder to release them. Energy is powerful, but you can reverse the effects of those subconscious beliefs that leave you feeling enslaved by combining visualization with a simple ritual to break those ties.

Three-Step Process

You can help to break any negative patterns that you have inherited with a simple three-step process. Take each step day by day, and if you feel yourself slipping into old habits or thoughts, bring your focus back to the three key words: Acknowledge, Accept, and Release.

STEP ONE: Acknowledge

Identify your family karma and acknowledge it. Being aware puts you in a position of power.

STEP TWO: Accept

Accept this is your karma and that you have the power to break the cycle and change it.

STEP THREE: Release

Release the karma by performing a ritual or simply breathe it out of your system as you exhale. Focus on letting it go from your body and mind.

"I break the cycle of karma, and I am released."

Releasing Negative Karma

Combine the cleansing power of visualization with crystal magic, to help you release any negative karma that you have been holding on to.

TRY THIS!
Cut the Ties

1. Make sure you give yourself enough time and space for this visualization. To begin, put some pillows/cushions on the floor and sit down. Spend a couple of minutes breathing deeply to calm and quieten your mind.
2. Take a pen and paper and think about the ancestral karma you have inherited. Write a couple of sentences or key words to sum this up. Focus on the root of the problem and the way it makes you feel—for example, "fear of change, lack of control." Fold the paper up and place it in front of you.
3. Hold the sodalite in both hands. This healing crystal transcends time to strengthen the bonds with your ancestors, while helping you move forward with clarity.
4. Close your eyes and picture yourself sitting in the center of a sacred circle. This could be a stone circle or one that has been drawn on the ground. Let your imagination take over and picture the space.
5. Breathe deeply and feel the healing energy that surrounds you. As you look down, you notice threads of golden light emerging from your body and stretching out into the distance. Each thread represents a belief or pattern of behavior that is specific to you and your family. You might notice that one seems stronger than all the others. Perhaps it is thicker, brighter, or a different color. This represents the negative karma that you need to release from your life.

"I am the author of my own tale."

6. At your feet you see a pair of silver scissors. Unlike ordinary scissors, these sparkle with healing light and are much more powerful. They are able to slice through any kind of karmic tie.

7. Pick the scissors up and when you're ready, cut through the karmic tie. Watch as the thread falls easily to your feet, where it is absorbed into the earth.

8. Notice how you feel now that the tie is cut. You might feel lighter and brighter inside.

9. To finish, say: "I cut the tie that brings me down, I bury it beneath the ground. I break the cycle with light and love and all good blessings from above."

10. Open your eyes and take the paper in one hand and the scissors in the other, then cut through the middle of the paper. Let the pieces of paper fall, then gather them up and discard them.

11. Keep the sodalite with you to boost the healing process and to help you look to the future with positivity.

YOU WILL NEED

Pillows/cushions, a piece of paper and pen, sodalite crystal, scissors

Ancestral Karma Meditation

Mindful breathing can be done at any time and anywhere. It's a useful tool for bringing you back to the present moment, to help shift your focus if you feel you're falling into negative thought patterns, and to enable you to progress the healing of your ancestral karma.

TRY THIS!
Breathing Exercise

1. Begin by focusing on your breathing, the gentle rise and fall of your chest, the path each breath takes as you inhale through the nose.
2. Follow the trail until the breath reaches your lungs. Notice how your chest expands and your stomach extends as your lungs inflate.
3. Release the breath slowly by exhaling through your mouth and notice how your stomach relaxes when you do this. See this as a continual loop, a circular cycle that energizes body and mind.
4. As you inhale, count to four slowly in your mind and do the same thing as you exhale.
5. Repeat this pattern of counting for a few more breaths, then extend this further by lengthening the inward and outward breath to five.
6. Now bring your attention to your feet and where you are standing. Feel the connection of your feet with the ground, and how this supports you. Imagine that as you draw in a breath, invisible cords of energy emerge from the sole of each foot and harness you to the earth. Feel the pull of these cords, as they secure you in place.
7. Every time you inhale, you draw in grounding energy from the earth, which travels into your feet, up each leg, and on to your stomach and chest.

8. As you exhale, you release any fear or anxiety and let it float up into the air where it will be transformed into positive energy.
9. Continue this breathing pattern for at least five minutes and try to maintain your focus by charting the journey of each breath and your connection to the earth.

"My ancestral karma motivates me to be the best version of myself."

The Gift of Karma

Karma of any kind is important. It's an opportunity to learn something about yourself and to accelerate your spiritual progression. Spells will help you work with and release any negative karma, so you can move forward with a positive mindset.

TRY THIS!

Karma Candle Spell

YOU WILL NEED

Two pillar candles of the same size (one black and one white), some sea salt

1. This spell is best performed when the moon is waning (getting smaller), but it can also be performed on a Full Moon, to boost the healing process.
2. Position the black and white candles next to each other on your ancestral altar (see page 82), or a table if you prefer. Light both candles.
3. Sprinkle the sea salt in a circle around both candles. Sea salt is renowned for its protective and cleansing properties.
4. Acknowledge any karma by saying, "I accept that the cycle of karma continues, and I see it as a gift from which I can learn and move forward."
5. Watch the two flames grow. Know that the black candle represents any negative karma, while the white symbolizes the light and new growth. Together they provide balance.
6. Take a deep breath in and blow out the flame of the black candle.
7. Next say, "I break any ties that hold me back. I accept the light and let it shine bright."
8. Now blow out the white candle.
9. Say, "I move forward and release the past."
10. Sit for a moment with your thoughts. Visualize a flame within your chest that grows bigger and brighter with every breath.

Further Healing Tools

The crystals, herbs, and scents listed below can be used to help you connect with your ancestral karma and to enhance any healing work you do.

Crystals to Carry and Meditate With

- Agate
- Amazonite
- Amber
- Opalite
- Sodalite
- Sunstone

Herbs and Plants

Burn in a fireproof bowl or infuse in hot water and inhale the plant's aroma.

- Aloe vera
- Basil
- Rosemary
- Sage
- Thyme
- Vetiver

Essential Oils and Incense

Burn some incense or use essential oils in an oil burner or add them to bath water.

- Bergamot
- Black pepper
- Eucalyptus
- Frankincense
- Lavender
- Mint

"I am healed with light and love."

More Healing Tips

Ancestral karma takes years to build up, and releasing it is an ongoing process. The following tips will complement any healing work that you do.

Be Kind

Be kind to yourself. If you feel that you are slipping back into old habits, don't judge or berate yourself. Instead, focus on the positive and acknowledge all the work you have done and will continue to do. Say to yourself: "I am doing well, and I will continue to make progress." Be kind to your ancestors too. They lived in different times, and their life experiences will likely have differed from your own. Don't fall into the trap of judging them for any habits or beliefs you have inherited. Try and put yourself in their shoes and consider how they might have felt or the challenges they faced.

Be Patient

Give yourself time and space to breathe. There is no quick fix. Healing ancestral karma is an ongoing process. Giving yourself time and space is key because it's a way of acknowledging that this is important to you. It also helps if you can allocate a regular time slot for working on this, perhaps at the end of the working week before your thoughts turn toward the weekend.

Be Aware

Go with the flow. Some days you will have more energy than others and feel more positive. Other days you may feel under the weather or vulnerable. Notice your moods and feelings, and work with them. Don't force yourself to address a family habit on a day when your energy is depleted or you are feeling vulnerable. When you are aware of yourself and how you feel, you accelerate the healing process by working with your body's natural rhythms.

Be Joyful

Enjoy the process. This might sound strange, but working with ancestral karma brings you closer to your ancestors. You are connecting with them at a deeper level, and that can be joyful. You'll learn more about them and yourself, which will help you empathize with them. It doesn't matter that you may not have known them, as taking the time to think about who they were and the habits you might have inherited will help you connect. It will also help you to feel secure and grounded in yourself. When you know and understand your roots, you can work toward strengthening them.

Be Proactive

Keep a record of your journey. It's easy to think that you're not making progress and to be hard upon yourself, when you have, in fact, made huge steps in the right direction. If you journal regularly, you'll be able to look back and see how far you have come. You'll also be able to use this space to reflect on and connect with your ancestors. Remember also to acknowledge your successes—those moments when you take a leap forward—or even more subtle achievements, such as simply being aware of your karma and accepting it. Give yourself a pat on the back and say, "I am enough!"

Be Positive

Create positive affirmations tailored to your ancestral karma. For example, if you feel that one of the beliefs you have inherited is related to a fear of change, then turn this on its head and make a positive statement like "I embrace change and go with the flow." Even if you feel that you are not doing this, simply stating it in a positive manner every day will help to align your thoughts and actions toward this way of being.

Be Present

Use your ancestral altar when you need some quiet time or a healing boost. Treat it as a sacred space where you can connect with your ancestors and enjoy spending time there. We so rarely allow ourselves the time just to sit and give thanks for who we are, or for our body and mind to recharge.

Be Forgiving

Make forgiveness your new superpower. Whatever you have learned about the ancestral karma that you've inherited, one of the best ways to heal and move forward is to forgive. This means forgiving those who went before. Remember, like you, they will have inherited certain beliefs and behaviors that they were not fully aware of. It also means forgiving yourself for any past mistakes, actions, words, and deeds. Know that you are doing your best to create good karma and to carry the wisdom of your ancestors with you.

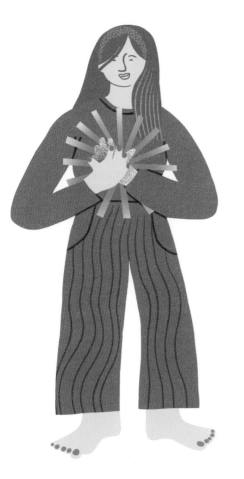

"The wisdom of my elders fuels good karma for the future."

Journal Exercise

Consider what you have learned about your ancestral karma and how you now feel after working through the rituals in this section. Do you feel stronger, lighter, brighter? Perhaps you are still trying to change your habits and beliefs. It can take a long time to work through the karma you've inherited, and it is an ongoing process. Be kind to yourself.

Think of three things that you can do to ease the process, from taking time out to reflect and looking after your health and wellbeing, to more practical things like sharing your thoughts with relatives. In your journal, make a note of these things and any others that come to mind. Make a point of introducing some of these suggestions into your daily schedule.

Get into the habit of checking in with yourself every day, noting how you feel and whether you have made any progress.

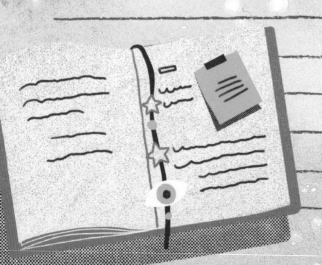

chapter FIVE

What's Your Familial Superpower(s)?

This chapter looks at the superpowers you have inherited from your ancestors. From qualities and strengths that run in the family, to latent skills and talents that emerge over time, your DNA is influenced by those who went before, which you'll discover as you strengthen those connections with your spiritual guides. You'll learn how to make the most of these superpowers and draw on them every day using rituals, techniques, and specially crafted affirmations.

"I look to the past
for my power."

What Is an Inherited Superpower?

To answer this question, you must first consider what is a superpower? Is it something otherworldly, a supernatural gift that brings out your inner hero and helps you to shine? Perhaps it's an inherent strength, something that carries you through the toughest times in your life? Or it could be a skill that you can put to good use, something that benefits others as well as yourself.

A superpower is all of these things and more. It doesn't have to be a "mystical" gift as such, but there is magic there: in the strength of your talent and the way that you use it. For example, if writing is your gift and you find it easy to put the right words together, then this can seem like a magical process. Should you take the time to write a poem for someone else, then this becomes a magical gift, not just in its making and shaping, but also in the way it makes that person feel. How you use your superpower can enhance it even more, and that's something worth thinking about once you've identified any gifts you have.

An inherited superpower is a gift, talent, or skill that has been passed down through the family line. Sometimes it skips a generation. Sometimes it takes a little digging to discover exactly what it is. The more you learn about your ancestors and how they lived, the more likely you are to draw those comparisons and uncover any latent abilities you might have. For example, you may learn—through asking questions of current family members and carrying out some of the earlier exercises in this book—that one of your ancestors was a talented artist. Maybe this is what they were known for, or it's something they enjoyed doing in their spare time, but never pursued further. This may strike a chord with your own life right now. Perhaps you loved art at school and had a talent for it, which you've let slide in adulthood, or maybe you still draw, but as a hobby. The idea of painting/drawing/sketching might appeal to you, even if you haven't tried it before. Simply hearing about your ancestor could be enough to pique your interest and you find that you can't stop thinking about it. These are all signs that this could be an inherited gift.

Your superpower could be something you consider to be a character trait. For example, you might discover that your ancestor was in business and then lost everything and went bankrupt. You may then learn that they made it through this challenge and started a new business and life elsewhere. These actions alone reveal a resilience and strength of character that you may identify with. Perhaps you can draw a comparison with your own life and how you have coped with adversity. It would be fair to say this is a superpower and something that has been passed down the family line.

Superpowers come in all shapes and sizes, just like family members. They can reveal themselves at any point during your Ancestral Magic journey, and you may already be aware of some of them. But even if you're not, there are simple steps you can take to discover your gifts and bring out your inner superhero.

Practical Steps

If you struggle with self-esteem, then uncovering your familial superpower might seem like a difficult task. You might think you have no particular skills, but if you take practical steps and approach it from an investigative stance, you'll soon identify qualities and strengths that others have been aware of for some time.

Start With You

This might seem obvious, but knowing yourself and who you are is the starting point in anything related to your family and any ancestral superpowers you may have inherited. You know yourself better than anyone, and this includes your natural skills and talents, even if you feel awkward acknowledging them. At a subconscious level you're probably aware of the gifts you've inherited and how to work with them, but the conscious mind takes over as you become occupied with the world around you. The key to uncovering your superpowers lies within you.

TRY THIS!
Who, What, Where, Why, When, and How?

Imagine you're a journalist on a fact-finding mission. You need to establish the facts, and to do this you can use a series of direct questions to uncover the truth. Answer them honestly and they will lead you there.

This exercise is quite lengthy, so make sure to have plenty of time, or take it in stages and address each of the questions separately. Open your journal and prepare to write the list of questions as they appear in the steps below. Allow one question per page, so you have lots of space to note down your thoughts. Answer each question in turn, writing down the first thing that comes to mind.

1. **Who am I?** Consider what makes you special and what is important to you. Let your thoughts flow and don't edit anything; simply allow your natural responses to fill the page.
2. **What am I good at?** List all things you do well, such as tidying, listening, and hugging, alongside more practical skills and talents like writing, cooking, singing, and so on.
3. **Where do I feel my best?** For example, you might feel that you really shine when you're the center of attention or working in a team at work, or perhaps you are at your best when you're at the heart of your family.
4. **Why do I feel this way?** What is it that makes you good at something? Perhaps it's something you have been doing for a long time, in which case you have the experience and

knowledge to make you feel confident, or maybe being with certain people gives you a sense of self-worth and the ability to unleash a particular skill or talent.

5. **When do I feel at my most powerful?** What time of day works for you and which type of environment do you need to truly excel? Perhaps you're a morning person, and need the quiet to flourish, or maybe you're a night owl who likes noise to unleash your creative side.

6. **How can I use all this information?** This is a big question, so you may need more than one page. Use what you've just discovered to step into your superpower. Remember, the process starts with baby steps, so try simple things like building confidence by practicing a skill or taking a course to further enhance your ability. Other ideas might be to spend time with others who make you feel comfortable and confident, mix with those who are experts at something that you're good at, work with mentors, and so on. Even small changes like giving yourself the freedom and time to explore some of your gifts by creating a window in your busy schedule are important.

It doesn't matter whether you write a lot or just have a few answers for each question. You can add more at any point. This is about unpicking the layers of who you are and the talents and gifts you've inherited. It's also the first step to helping you see your potential and how you might make the most of your superpowers.

Ask Family and Friends

Your family and friends know you better than anyone else, so if you're struggling to come up with a list of skills and gifts, they'll be able to help you. Petition your family and friends and ask them what they like about you and what they feel are your strengths and talents. Even if you disagree with the things they suggest, add them to your list of potential superpowers. Those who know us can be more objective and will see things that we often miss.

Go Back to Childhood

What were you good at in school? Get out your old school report cards and read what the teachers said. Were there any subjects you excelled in or found easy? Even comments that might have seemed negative at the time can highlight particular skills. For example, your teacher may have said you were a chatterbox or the class clown, which means you had a gift for communication and boosting morale.

Also consider what you enjoyed doing as a child. Perhaps you loved painting and drawing or playing sport. There are often clues to be found if we look back in time and consider the things that were important to us when we were much younger. Time, and the demands of the adult world, can steer us away from our true calling and even dull the gifts we've been given. So, by looking back we can identify those early influences and talents that we inherited and then develop them further.

Make Family Connections

When you look at the list of talents and skills you have identified so far, do any stand out as being common within your family grouping? Perhaps you have a gift for crafts and making things, and this is something you share with another family member. Maybe you've heard that your great-grandmother could turn her hand to making anything from scratch, and you seem to have inherited the same ability. It makes sense then that this is an inherited superpower, and that your great-grandmother got this gift from her parents or even further back. Spend some time making those connections by looking at what you already know about those closest to you.

> "I am powerful, talented, and ready for anything!"

Delve into Your Desires

Take some time to indulge your desires. What are you drawn to? What brings you joy and, if you had all the time and money in the world, what would you like to do? The answers to these questions can reveal latent skills or talents that have yet to be developed. You might also identify a gift that runs in the family. Perhaps you'd love to fly a plane and you have no idea why, but it's something you've always wanted to try. On further digging and asking questions of current family members, you might discover that your great-grandfather had an interest in planes— maybe he was an engineer or flew planes in a war? Don't discard any of your impulses or dreams, as they are often based in reality, and there is always a reason why we are drawn to certain pursuits.

Build Ancestral Profiles

Use what you already know about your ancestors to reveal the skill connections between you (see page 104).

A New Perspective

1. Pick an ancestor that you know something about and build a picture of their character and who they were.
2. Write your ancestor's name in your journal and make a list of what you know about them.
3. Think about their likes and dislikes, as well as the things they must have been good at and enjoyed doing. Look at old photographs for clues—you might have a picture of them in their garden or in a community garden (allotment), which suggests they were skilled at growing things.
4. Consider what this ancestor did for a living and what it reveals about them. For example, did they work with their hands? Perhaps they had their own business, which implies they were good at business and had a drive to succeed.
5. Consider the type of qualities your ancestor would have needed to excel in their field of interest. Did they work with other people? Perhaps they had staff or were part of a team? What does this reveal about who they were and what they were good at?
6. Write a summary of your deductions and highlight any key traits, talents, or gifts that you recognize within yourself by circling them.
7. You can repeat this exercise with other ancestors and even family members who you know well. It will help you look at them from a different perspective, and you'll probably discover things that will strengthen your existing relationships.

"The magic of the past blesses my present."

Ancestral Gifts Visualization

Your ancestral guides will be more than happy to help you discover your inherited superpowers. After all, they've given you these gifts to use, so it makes sense to call on them for help. You can do this in a number of ways, from asking out loud or through meditation, or you could write down your request and leave it on your ancestral altar. Another effective way to garner their attention and help is through visualization. If you have already used this tool successfully to connect with certain ancestors, then why not use it again to communicate with them on this issue.

TRY THIS!

Reflect Your Inner Superhero

Make yourself comfortable and find a space where you won't be disturbed. Switch off your phone and create a relaxing atmosphere. You might want to light some candles, play background music, or burn some scented essential oil or incense.

1. Close your eyes and focus on your breathing. Pay attention to the rise and fall of your chest and take long, deep breaths to clear your mind.
2. When you're ready, begin the visualization (see opposite).
3. Now bring your attention back to your breathing and spend a few minutes acclimatizing by focusing on the rise and fall of your chest.
4. Slowly become more aware of your surroundings and open your eyes.
5. Stretch your body and legs and take a few deep breaths in through the nose and out through the mouth.
6. Be sure to spend at least five minutes running through the visualization in your mind and make any notes of things that stand out in your journal. Reflect on what you have learned.

The Visualization

Imagine you are standing in front of a door. It can be any type of door, from ornate to a simple wooden structure; it's entirely up to you and your imagination. You turn the handle and enter a room with lights in all the corners. The decor is opulent, and while there isn't much in the way of furniture, there is a tall, freestanding mirror in the center of the room. It's covered by a length of dark fabric. You walk slowly toward the mirror and stand before it. You take a long, deep breath and pull the fabric away to reveal the beautiful golden mirror. As you peer at your reflection, you notice shadows gathering around you, but rather than being ominous, these shapes are warm and comforting, and you recognize them to be your ancestors. They are here to support you and reveal your gifts to you. You may want to take a moment to thank them for their presence.

When you're ready, turn your attention back to yourself and your mirror image. How do you look? You may look different to how you expected. Perhaps you are dressed in something new or your reflection is distorted. You reach out with your hand toward the glass and, as you do, a beam of light shoots into the mirror and your reflection becomes clear and vibrant, as if you've stepped into your power. Now is the time to ask about the talents you have inherited. You may receive a gift from one of the gathered ancestors or you may hear a voice. You may see something in your reflection that hints at your latent powers, or perhaps you simply know the answer and feel it inside. Let this insight come to you, in whatever way feels natural. Don't force it and don't worry if nothing happens. It may be that this visualization is just the starting point and that the answers you are seeking will come after this, in the form of signs and synchronicities.

When you are ready and feel you have learned enough, thank your ancestors for being there with you. Place the fabric cover over the mirror once more and return through the door.

Altar Meditation

Meditation can help you go within and uncover your superpowers. It helps to rid the mind of constant chatter and will calm and quieten thoughts, so you can hear your inner voice. How you choose to meditate is up to you, but it's a good idea to use the tools available to you, so set some time aside to sit by your ancestral altar and make your intention known—light a candle and say a few words to state your aim.

TRY THIS!

Sit in Stillness

1. Set the scene and create a relaxing atmosphere. Also make sure to allow yourself plenty of time for this exercise.
2. Dab a couple of drops of lavender essential oil onto your pulse points and also rub a little into the middle of your forehead where your Third Eye chakra is located. This energy point helps you connect with your higher self and allows your intuition to flow.
3. Make yourself comfortable, sitting on plenty of pillows or cushions or, if you prefer, use a yoga mat.
4. Close your eyes and let your body relax. Roll your shoulders back and soften your chest.
5. Slow down your breathing by counting each breath you draw in. Hold the breath for an extra count, then release slowly through your mouth.
6. Focus on this breathing pattern and tune out from the outside world. If thoughts come into your mind, simply acknowledge them and bring your awareness back to your breathing.
7. At some point over the course of this meditation, you will notice peace descending. You will feel a moment of pure stillness as your mind sits in silence with itself. Be aware of this moment and embrace it.
8. Imagine freezing time at this point and holding onto the stillness. See it as a white light that you hold within your mind. Let the light fill you up and focus solely on the peaceful sensations that you experience. The world goes on around you, but you are completely detached.
9. You may notice thoughts knocking at the door of your mind, and that is fine. You may also experience a vision or hear a voice within. Let these things play out in your head.

10. It is during these moments of complete stillness that you are most likely to hear your inner voice. Your intuition will finally have the room to speak to you, and if you set the intention before you began of identifying any gifts that have been passed down your ancestral line, then these will likely come to light. Even if this doesn't happen, just sit, relax, and enjoy the peaceful moment.

11. When you are ready, bring your focus back to your breathing and begin to count out each breath, as you did when you first began the meditation.

12. Slowly become aware of any external sounds, such as the wind outside your window or traffic noises. Adjust your attention and, when you are ready, open your eyes.

13. Don't rush headlong into chores or activities, but give your body and mind time to catch up. It's not often that we truly sit in stillness and go within, so reflect upon this exercise. If you recall anything from the experience, note it down in your journal.

YOU WILL NEED

Lavender essential oil, pillows/cushions or a yoga mat, journal and pen

"My ancestors work through me in all I do."

Candle Magic

A simple spell using candle magic can send a powerful message to your higher self. This is where your subconscious mind is in control. Your intuition will naturally respond to this call to arms over the next few days and send you clues and signs that reveal your inherited gifts.

TRY THIS!
Your Inherited Gifts

YOU WILL NEED

White candle, pin, piece of paper and a pen, fireproof bowl

This spell is best performed when the moon is waning (getting smaller), as it will help you go within for answers.

1. Take the white candle and use the pin to carve your initials into the wax.
2. Light the candle and say, "I cast this light upon my soul, the answers I seek are my goal."
3. Take the pen and paper and write down the question: "What gifts have I inherited from my ancestors?"
4. Pass the paper through the candle flame and cast it into the bowl. Let it burn away to ash.
5. Sit quietly and watch the flame flicker for a few minutes. Let your mind wander and allow any thoughts to come and go.
6. When you're ready, take the bowl outside and scatter the ash into the wind.
7. Repeat the words from earlier: "I cast this light upon my soul, the answers I seek are my goal."
8. Over the next few days, be open and aware of any messages or intuitive signs and keep journaling your thoughts. Also take note of your dreams as they may also include clues.

Become a Superhero

Every superhero needs a little time and practice to get into full swing, especially when they've just discovered a new power, and it's the same for you. You might suddenly be aware of a new talent or skill that you have inherited, but it will take patience and time to develop. The key is to set yourself a target and create a training plan. Treat it like a fitness regime, where you build up strength and stamina, and outline a series of steps and mini goals that are achievable for you.

For example, if you feel that you have musical ability, then your first step would be to identify which instrument you're drawn to and learn as much about it as possible. You might then decide to get some lessons to help you play the instrument as the next step in your plan. After a couple of months of lessons, you might decide to set yourself a small challenge, such as playing to a group of friends. This would be a mini goal. Once you have hit this target, you could explore bigger challenges or ways in which you can enhance your musical ability and perfect what you have learned, perhaps by taking tests or even joining a musical group.

In some cases, the skills or talents that you have inherited may already be quite advanced, but you didn't realize or put them to the back of your mind. If this is the case, then you might be able to skip the first couple of steps and work on enhancing the gifts you have. It's about assessing what you know and where you are at. Also, some powers are more inherent to your personality and how you relate to others. For example, you may be a gifted empath, in which case your skill comes naturally, and this is about learning to control and work with it.

"I embrace the gifts I have been given."

Superhero Practice

The answers to the following questions and prompts will help you create a plan that works for you and your current situation:

- What is your gift?
- How much do you know about it?
- Are you a complete beginner or is this something you have been aware of for a while?
- Identify three things you could do to learn about your superhero power.
- Are you able to incorporate this new gift into your life right now? For example, do you have other commitments and would you need to set some time aside for this?
- Identify a time during the week when you can explore your new skill.
- Do you know anyone who could help you with your gift? A mentor? A teacher? A guide? If not, look into ways of meeting like-minded people who can assist you.
- What can you do to enhance your gift?
- How could others benefit from this inherited power? For example, if you're good with figures and calculations, perhaps you could offer your accounting skills to a charity that means a lot to you, or, if your power is that you're a good listener, maybe you could volunteer for a helpline or train to be a counselor. What you decide to do will depend on your answers to the previous questions.

"I let my inner superhero shine."

Ask Your Ancestors

Now you have discovered the inherited superpowers that have been passed down through your family line, you can turn to your ancestors for advice on how to develop and use these skills.

Go Within

1. Sit at your ancestral altar (see page 82) and imagine you are addressing your ancestral guides.
2. To begin, thank them for the gifts you have been given, then ask them to show you how to work with these powers.
3. Close your eyes and go within. Let the silence surround you and allow any thoughts to come and go. Don't be tempted to force anything, just relax and enjoy taking five minutes out of your busy schedule.

Devote some time to this simple ritual every day. Remember to repeat the process of thanking your ancestors and asking for guidance, then close your eyes for a few minutes and let the thoughts flow.

Trust that your ancestors will support and guide you through your intuition. Over time, you will receive wisdom in the form of a sudden burst of inspiration, an idea, or a recurring thought that spurs you into action.

Journal Exercise

Consider everything you have learned about yourself since working through the exercises in this chapter. Do you have a clearer idea of your gifts and strengths, and how these things connect you to your ancestors? Perhaps you feel closer to them, now that you realize you share certain talents and traits. Does acknowledging these gifts make you feel more confident and empowered? If not, why?

In your journal, make a definitive list of your superpowers and read through it. Certain gifts will stand out more than others. Perhaps this is because you use them more in your everyday life or maybe you feel more confident about certain abilities. Maybe you have received praise in the past for these particular talents, and that has re-enforced your self-belief. Highlight them in some way and consider why they are important to you. Jot down your thoughts.

Now think about the other items on your list. Pick one and write it as a heading on a separate journal page. Consider the ways in which you can develop this gift. Think about practical things you can do to enhance it and set yourself a time limit. For example, if one of your gifts is gardening, and you'd like to develop this skill, you might offer to tidy and landscape a neighbor's garden over the next month. You have now set yourself a challenge and given yourself a timeframe to work to. You can then reflect upon this when you have finished and see if it made a difference to how your feel about this gift.

What's Your Family Totem and Other Talismans?

This chapter looks at a variety of magical tools and techniques that you can use to harness the power and protection of your ancestors. You'll learn how you can call upon your own spiritual tag team for strength, support, and encouragement, as well as how to use those connections from the past to anchor you in the present moment. You'll also discover practical ways for maintaining those ancestral connections on a daily basis and how to use spells, rituals, talismans, and charms to harness the magic within you.

"Family treasures keep me connected and strong."

Everyday Ancestral Magic

Every time you reach out to your ancestors, you perform a magical feat. You are expending energy in the hope of connecting with the spiritual realm to achieve a desired outcome. Each meditation and visual narrative that you use is a magical tool to bring you closer together, and there are so many other more practical things you can do to work with your ancestors. From asking for their support and protection to harnessing their latent gifts, you can use their gathered strength to generate positive energy, which boosts abundance, attracts more love, and can even turn your family's fortunes around.

While this may sound unbelievable, the fact is that you can do this every day, with a few simple tricks and tweaks that will change the way you think and act. Ancestral Magic is as much about attitude as anything else. Get into the habit of using the techniques and rituals within this section on a daily basis, and you will feel more empowered and connected to your family, past and present.

"I take to heart the values that are important to my family."

Start Each Day

Get into a positive and magical frame of mind, so you can connect with your ancestors throughout the day, every day.

TRY THIS!

Morning Mirror Magic

1. On rising, stand in front of a mirror. Look yourself in the eye, smile, and greet yourself like an old friend.
2. Say, "Hello, beautiful you! Today I am open and ready to draw upon the strength of my ancestors. I take every opportunity to let my innate magic flow."
3. Now repeat the statement with feeling. Imagine you're putting it out there to the Universe, so be loud and proud. Draw a breath from your belly and project each word as if you want the entire street to hear you.
4. Say the statement a third time and really make it count. Think about each word and what it means as you say it.
5. Smile and return to your normal routine.

Spells and Rituals

As you delve deeper into your ancestry, and learn about those who went before, you will develop rituals and techniques to harness their power. This is a natural process and you might not be aware of it at first.

Simple things such as taking a moment to still your mind, then addressing your ancestors as if they're in the room with you, are rituals that often go unnoticed. They become a routine part of your practice and something that you do automatically to create the right ambience. Spells are also a part of this. Every time you set your intention to connect with your ancestors and reach out for guidance, you are casting a spell. You have established your desire and followed this through with an action such as meditating, visualization, or lighting a candle and writing down your questions, and just like magic, you believe in the outcome.

You know that your ancestors will speak to you through your intuition. In effect, you have created a spell to help you succeed. This is why it's so important to maintain your journal. If you keep this updated, and record every experience you have, you'll discover which rituals and spells work for you. You'll recognize the elements needed to make them effective and your confidence will grow. You'll also be able to mix and match, creating your own spells and rituals and personalizing your Ancestral Magic. Remember, this is your family history and they are your ancestors—you are at the center of everything—so it's important to make your practice unique to you. You're more likely to see positive results when you customize techniques to suit you and your family.

TRY THIS!

Ritual Experiment

1. Go back through your journal and highlight any rituals, techniques, and mantras that you enjoyed. Perhaps a certain ritual held meaning for you, or you achieved surprising results. Circle these and read through the details.
2. Identify the parts that you particularly enjoyed. What can you take from this and how might you adapt it to create your own personal spell or ritual?
3. Have a go at picking two or three elements from all the practices you have highlighted and putting them together to create a new ritual.
4. Write down each step of the process, then set some time aside to experiment and see if the ritual works.
5. It doesn't matter if things don't go to plan or you don't achieve positive results. This is about trying something new to see if it feels right. You'll soon get to know what works for you and find yourself naturally creating spells and rituals that you can work with.

"The power and wisdom of my ancestors surrounds me every day."

Ancestral Spells

To help you on your Ancestral Magic journey, here are some fun spells that are easy to incorporate into your daily routine. These are only suggestions, and you may want to adapt them to suit your needs or use them as a basis for creating your own spells and rituals.

TRY THIS!

Spell to Generate Joy

Fill your life with happiness by calling on your ancestors for help. This easy spell will show you how to generate joy by reconnecting with the past.

1. You're going to make a fruit pie in honor of your ancestors. First, grease the pie dish and then line with the premade pastry (reserving enough for the pastry top). Add the fruit filling to the dish, making sure it's level. Cover with the remaining pastry. Have fun with this process and be creative. You might, for example, want to make some sort of pastry decoration for the topping. Infuse the pie with love and attention. It doesn't matter if the pie isn't perfect, as this is all about the process of creating and baking something. Bake the pie in the oven, on a medium to high heat for approximately 40–45 minutes, or until golden brown.
2. While the pie is baking, take the pen and paper and write down a wish for joy. Make this something simple, such as "I wish for the happiness to flow in my life."
3. Bring your ancestors to mind and ask them to help you with this. Say, "Please help me appreciate the blessings in my world and find the joy in everything I do."
4. Spend this time thinking about all the things that have made you happy in the past. Run through those memories and let them fill you with joy.
5. When the pie is ready, remove it from the oven and let cool. You can either eat a piece every day to remind you to take a moment of pleasure, or give your piece away to someone you care for as a way of spreading joy and creating more positive energy.

YOU WILL NEED

Pie dish, butter for greasing, some premade shortcrust pastry, a fruity filling of your choice, some paper and a pen

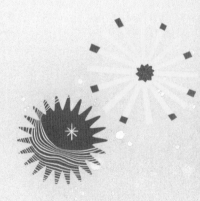

TRY THIS!

Spell to Feel the Love

This spell is like a giant ancestral cuddle, and it will draw your ancestors close and help you feel loved.

1. To begin, create a loving atmosphere by lighting the candles.
2. Put the pink flowers in the vase with some water, then place them on your ancestral altar (see page 82).
3. Pour a tablespoon of almond oil into the dish. Add three drops of geranium essential oil, which helps to balance the emotions and boost self-love. Mix slowly with your index finger.
4. Close your eyes, then use your fingers to gently massage a little of the scented oil into the middle of your chest in a circular motion. This is where your Heart chakra resides, the energy center associated with your emotions.
5. As you do this, ask your ancestors to draw close and support you. Say, "I give and receive love freely."
6. Finally, wrap the blanket around your shoulders and feel the warmth of its caress.
7. Imagine your ancestors surrounding you, and feel them draw you in for a loving embrace.

YOU WILL NEED

Candles, pink flowers and a vase, tablespoon, almond oil, small dish, geranium essential oil, cozy blanket

"My family's magic runs through my veins."

Ancestral Abundance Spell

Enlist the help of your ancestors to boost your finances and attract abundance into your home.

YOU WILL NEED

Old family photograph, empty jar with a lid, selection of silver coins

1. Take the photograph—this could be a childhood picture or one that's even older, as long as it links you to the past and your family—and place it in the jar.
2. Cover the photograph with a handful of silver coins to represent financial success.
3. Put the lid on the jar and give it a shake. Then say, "Ancestral abundance down the line, the gift of prosperity passed through time. The money I need, and more to come, and so I am blessed with a healthy sum."
4. Leave the jar by your front door.
5. Whenever you leave home, throw in your loose change in the jar. Then when you return, give the jar a shake and repeat the magical chant.

TRY THIS!

Spell to Call on Your Ancestors for Support

YOU WILL NEED
Dining table, tablecloth, place mats, cutlery and glasses, large white candle

Imagine you're throwing a dinner party for your ancestors. You might have specific relatives in mind or just a general idea of who might be at your table.

This spell will help you connect with the strength and wisdom of your ancestors. If you're feeling alone and vulnerable, it will help you connect with your family, past and present.

1. Begin by setting the table as you would normally if guests were coming. Cover with a tablecloth and place mats and set out the cutlery and glasses. Don't skimp on the niceties. Go for your best decor to help your ancestors feel special. Position the candle in the middle of the table and light it.
2. Take your place at the table and pour yourself a drink. Raise your glass and make the following toast, "Welcome, one and all, I invite your presence near. I call on your assistance and your comfort. May they be felt here. I open my heart to you and ask you do the same. Together as a family, as we sit around the flame."
3. Take a sip of your drink and a moment to enjoy the stillness.
4. Close your eyes and let any thoughts flow into your mind. Feel the presence of your ancestral guides. If you have any specific needs, voice them now.
5. Breathe in strength and breathe out fear.
6. When you're ready, open your eyes and thank your ancestors for visiting you.
7. To finish, extinguish the flame.

TRY THIS!
Ancestral Good Fortune Spell

This spell will help you generate positive energy and turn your luck around.

YOU WILL NEED

Some outside space, couple of slices of stale bread, bowl or bag, selection of stones

1. Before you go outside, take the bread and crumble it into tiny pieces. As you feel the crumbs between your fingers, think of all the thousands of blessings in your life. Bring to mind the wonderful moments you have had with your family, past and present, and all the brilliant people in your life right now.
2. Put the crumbs in a bowl or bag and go outside.
3. Position the stones in a large circle on the ground.
4. Once the stones are in place, begin to walk around the circle in a clockwise direction and scatter the breadcrumbs. As you do this, say out loud or in your head: "The wheel of fortune spins for me, as it always has for my family. The highs, the lows, they come around, and once again good luck is found."
5. When you've finished scattering the breadcrumbs, stand in the middle of the circle and take a minute to focus on your breathing. Feel the swell of energy as your lungs fill with air. Notice the cycle of each breath, the constant pattern of in and out, and how, like the wheel of life and your luck, everything has its moment.
6. Now think of your ancestors and how they too would have experienced the highs and lows of life. Maybe they weren't as fortunate as you, but they still found the power to move forward, embrace each day, and go with the flow.
7. Repeat the magical chant one more time, before stepping out of the circle.

Find Your Talisman

A talisman is an object that is imbued with spiritual power and significance. It is used to guide and protect an individual and to attract good luck.

Usually a sacred object, a talisman is something of value and meaning to the owner. It works like a lucky charm and helps to generate positive energy. Talismans can be passed down the generations, or they can be something new that you keep with you to represent the family group as a whole. As long as the talisman is special and serves to remind you of the connection that you have with your ancestors, then it holds power.

Ancestral Charm

A charm is something you can carry with you at all times. It provides a direct link between you and your ancestors, so you never need feel alone. Simply by holding the charm, you'll be able to draw on their combined energy to feel empowered and protected.

TRY THIS!

Presence, Protection, and Power

YOU WILL NEED

Small charm of your choice, quartz crystal, black scarf, sea salt

1. To begin, you need to identify something that can be the ancestral charm. It helps if the object has a direct link to your family, whether that's an immediate relative or further back. Something small and easy to keep about your person makes the ideal charm, so perhaps a piece of jewelry like a ring, brooch, or pin. It might be a family heirloom, such as a pocket watch or lucky coin, or just an item that belonged to someone close to you.

2. Once you have chosen the object, you need to cleanse it of any residual energy that it has picked up and charge it for your purpose. To do this, place the charm with the quartz crystal in the center of the scarf. The crystal will help to cleanse the object and charge it with powerful energy. Sprinkle over a pinch of sea salt for protection, then tie the scarf into a bundle. Leave this on your ancestral altar (see page 82) overnight.

3. In the morning, retrieve the scarf and remove the charm. Sit holding the object in front of your altar. Close your eyes and call upon your ancestors for assistance by saying something like: "I call upon your power and strength. I ask you to imbue this object with your energy so that I may feel your presence at all times and connect with your wisdom and grace."

4. Take a deep breath in and, as you breathe out, pour all that positive energy and your intention into the charm.

5. Repeat this breath pattern twice more, to charge the object with ancestral power.

6. When you've finished, keep the charm with you or leave it on your altar to recharge. Carry your charm for protection and hold it whenever you're feeling vulnerable.

Totems

Totems have been used for thousands of years and in a wide variety of cultures. They're an emblem, usually a sacred symbol or a specific creature, that represents a group or tribe of people. Highly symbolic, the totem represents the shared beliefs and values of that particular clan, and as such acts as a tie, bringing the group together, which in turn gives the totem energy and the power to affect an individual from that group. It reminds them of who they are and what's important. It also provides a spiritual crux, which can be called upon for strength and protection.

Ancestral Totems

While totems are usually associated with larger groups, they can also be ancestral and passed down through the ages from generation to generation. Sometimes they exist on a smaller scale within a family unit. While you may not think your family has its own totem, you could find that as you dig a little deeper and ask questions, a symbol rises to the surface. For example, you might discover that a particular place is important to your family, perhaps a castle or historic building. On further investigation, you find it features in your family history and that members of your family were often drawn to this place, particularly when they needed to recharge. Over time, this place has become a seat of strength and a symbol of resilience. The castle has become your family totem, and this can be represented in a number of ways. You might have a picture or photograph of it in your home or carry a piece of its stone with you. Maybe your connection is through the power of narrative, and you've collected stories associated with the place, which you share with members of your family. With time, the castle becomes a recognized totem that you carry with you, and a place to which you can return when you need to lift your spirits.

"The threads that connect me
to the past infuse me with energy."

TRY THIS!
Play Detective

YOU WILL NEED

Paper and pen, candles, pictures and objects that represent your totem

1. You can discover if your family has a totem with a little digging. Consider what you have learned about your ancestors so far. Does a place, an object, or even an animal seem to feature in your family folklore? Perhaps you've heard tales about it, or it seems to crop up in conversation. There might be more than one contender, so make a list, then take each one and write down what you know about it.

2. How many family members have mentioned this totem to you? How many times has it come up in conversation? Is it something you already knew about? Get all the facts down on paper.

3. Now spend some time sitting at your ancestral altar (see page 82). Light candles, if you wish, and do a simple breathing exercise such as the one on page 88–89, to calm your mind.

4. Look at what you have written and consider how you feel when you bring each place/object/creature to mind. What does each one mean to you? Does it make you feel connected to your ancestors? Perhaps you feel stronger, brighter, and more energized when you think about it, or maybe it helps to calm your nerves and center you.

5. As you work through your list, you will naturally be drawn to certain entries. They will feel right. This is your intuition speaking through your body and mind, and letting you know that this is your family totem.

6. Remember to ask your ancestors for guidance. They will help you uncover the truth.

7. Once you have established your totem, make it a feature of your ancestral altar in some way. Add pictures or objects to represent it. You might also want to carry a reminder of your totem with you, something that helps you connect with its power. Trust your instincts and use this emblem to empower you and bring you closer to your family, past and present.

Totem Power

You can use your totem to help you achieve goals and attract new opportunities. It will remind you of the key traits and talents you have inherited, while also boosting your self-worth and confidence.

Totem Practice

Try the following hints and suggestions for working with your ancestral totem:

- Learn as much as you can about your totem, so read books, go online and do some digging, ask questions, and build a picture in your mind.
- If your ancestral totem is a place, then you can visit and experience its power first-hand. Make memories there that you can draw on when you need a boost.
- Get creative. You can tap into the energy of the totem by unleashing your artistic side. Write a poem or story that includes your totem. Draw or paint a picture inspired by it. Or create a representation by getting "crafty." For example, you might want to have a go at knitting, weaving, sculpting, or sewing the totem.
- Find and play a piece of music that makes you think about your totem. Treat this like a theme tune, so whenever you need to think or feel positively, bring the song to mind and be reminded of your totem and the energy associated with it.
- Work the totem into a daily meditation. As you breathe and quieten your mind, concentrate on an image or representation of the totem. Make this the focus of the exercise and tune into its energy.

Protection Techniques

Ancestral Magic has many benefits, but one of its main uses is to anchor you to the past, to provide a sense of belonging, so you feel protected and guided at all times. This can be incredibly empowering, particularly if you're feeling vulnerable or facing challenges in life. To help you strengthen those ties with your past, and feel strong and supported, you can use a number of protection techniques.

TECHNIQUE
Grow Your Roots

This technique is perfect for those moments when you need courage. Perhaps you need to speak out, express how you feel, or take control of a situation. To help you feel secure, perform this visualization. Do this regularly if you want to maintain a strong connection with your ancestors and feel empowered.

1. Stand or sit, then bring your attention to the soles of your feet. Feel their connection with the ground.
2. Roll your feet from heel to toe and feel the floor beneath you.
3. Draw in a breath and, as you do, imagine tiny roots bursting from your feet and pushing deep into the earth.
4. As you exhale, the roots travel farther underground, anchoring you in place. Feel the strength of those roots securing you in place.
5. Continue to breathe deeply and visualize a tangle of roots bursting from the center of your chest. Like tiny threads of light, they spin in every direction. These threads travel beyond time and space into the spiritual realm. They connect you to your ancestors.
6. As you inhale, you draw in energy that flows along each thread and eventually fills your chest with warmth.
7. Continue to focus on the roots beneath your feet and those that tie you to your ancestors.
8. Know that you can move in any direction, but you will always feel these connections. They keep you balanced and focused.

TECHNIQUE
Family Circle

This technique is a visualization that can be performed anywhere. It will help you feel protected by your ancestors and able to assert and express yourself. It's the prefect exercise for when you need to stand your ground and make a statement.

1. To begin, draw your attention to your breathing. Still your mind of any internal chatter and negative thoughts by focusing on your breath.
2. Imagine each breath as a stream of fire that travels through your body, infusing you with power and strength. As you release this breath, it pours from your mouth in a fusion of flames, allowing you to unleash and offload any negative emotions.
3. Now imagine that as you stand on the spot, you are surrounded by your closest ancestral guides. They gather around you to form a tight circle.
4. You don't have to see the faces of your ancestors; they are a collection of cloaked beings who radiate an inner light and have your best interests at heart.
5. For every breath you take, more and more ancestors join the circle in layers that spread outward.
6. Soon you have a multitude of spiritual beings crowding around you. They provide layers of protection, but there are plenty of gaps offering breathing space and the capacity for you to move freely and speak your mind.
7. The circle moves with you, as you breathe. It supports you and provides a flow of energy, to help you assert yourself with confidence.
8. To finish, draw in a breath from the roots of the earth and feel the fiery flames light you up from the inside.
9. Exhale and release any tension from your body.
10. When you're ready, let your ancestors drift away one by one, but remember that you can call upon the group at any time when you feel vulnerable.

TECHNIQUE
Cloak of Power

This technique can help you feel strong and protected throughout the day. It's a simple breathing exercise combined with a visualization, which you can perform in the morning to help you connect to your ancestral guides.

1. Stand in front of a mirror and assess your posture. Take a long breath in and draw it through your body. As you do this, lengthen you spine and roll your shoulders back. Tilt you chin upward slightly and look into your eyes.
2. As you exhale, relax and smile.
3. Say, "May the power and strength of my ancestors boost my vitality."
4. Continue with this breathing pattern for a couple of minutes. Focus on drawing the breath through your body, so that you feel energized.
5. When you are ready, close your eyes and imagine you are standing with your ancestors. Feel the warmth of their energy wrap around you like a soft blanket.
6. Each time you inhale, feel the glow infusing you with power. Picture it as a golden cloak of light that cocoons you from head to toe. It protects you from negative energy, shielding your mind, body, and spirit, so that you remain centered.
7. Open your eyes, stand tall, and assess your posture once more. Do you notice any difference in your stance and expression?
8. Breathe deeply and relax.
9. Say, "The cloak of my ancestors shields and protects me at all times."

TECHNIQUE
Face-to-Face

This quick visualization is perfect for some on-the-spot protection.
If you're feeling vulnerable and just need a little boost, this can help.

1. Bring to mind one of your ancestors. Choose someone who you know a little about, to help you make that connection quickly. You might already have an idea of what they looked like or have a photograph, making it easy for you to picture them in your mind. Remember too that this could be a family member who you met and know well, who is now in spirit, like a grandparent.
2. Bring to mind your ancestor's face and imagine they are standing in front of you. What do you think they would say to you, right now? What words of encouragement would they use to bolster your spirit? Let them speak into your mind or, if you prefer, simply hold the vision of their face in your head.
3. Imagine your ancestor reaching out to you, holding your hand, or embracing you.
4. Breathe in the energy and strength your ancestor is sending.

Ancestral Mantras and Affirmations

Mantras and affirmations work with the power of language and sound, to help you harness certain abilities, skills, and emotions. They can switch up your thinking and help you connect with your ancestral guides, by focusing the mind and your energy. They're a practical magical tool that you can work with every day.

Mantras

Mantras are a word, melodic phrase, or sound that you can use to enhance any meditation. The choice of word(s) depends on what you're hoping to achieve. For instance, you could be seeking soothing energy for healing, so you might choose to repeat the word "peace," but if you're hoping to boost positivity, you might choose to focus on words like "joy," "light," and "love."

TRY THIS!
Strengthen Your Spiritual Connections

To help you work with your ancestors, repeat this simple mantra every morning and evening.

1. To begin, find somewhere comfortable to sit. Relax your body and close your eyes. If you can, sit cross-legged and let your hands rest palms upward on your lap. This open posture allows the energy to flow.
2. Take a long breath in and, as you exhale, let your jaw drop and make an "ahhhhh" sound. Draw this deep from your belly, so that it's low and resonates within. You should feel a gentle vibration in your chest.
3. Hold the sound for as long as possible, letting it peter out naturally.
4. Each time you take a breath, make the "ahhhhh" sound and feel your body vibrate with power.
5. Focus on steadily building this energy and imagine that with every breath you are turning up your shine, so that your guides in the spiritual realm can see and hear you. Do this for five minutes.
6. By the end of the session you should feel lighter, brighter, and in a positive frame of mind.

Affirmations

Affirmations are a statement of fact, said in the present tense to make the sentiment real. For example, if you want to feel happy, you could say, "Today I will be joyful." But this puts the action of being joyful in the future and places distance between you and your desire. However, if you say, "Today I am joyful," you bring your desire into the present moment and make it real.

You can create affirmations for anything, from the way you'd like to feel to what you'd like to manifest in your life. The key is to describe what you'd like and how you want to feel, then to put all your effort and belief into repeating this, as often as you can.

Affirmations work because they help to reprogram the way you think and feel. Like attracts like in the spiritual realm, so when you repeat an affirmation and believe in it, you create the positive energy to draw it into your life.

Affirmation Tips

- Look in the mirror as you say your affirmation and make eye contact with yourself. This can be difficult at first, but once you get into the habit, you'll see what a difference it makes to the strength of your affirmations and the outcome.

- Take a deep breath in and imagine you're projecting your affirmation to the back of the room. Don't be shy about this. Affirmations help to awaken your inner power, by allowing you to express yourself freely.

- Inject as much energy into each word of the affirmation as you can, and really think about the sentiment behind it.

- Repeat the affirmation in sets of three or more. This gives your brain time to catch up, and by the third or fourth attempt you'll really be behind every word.

- As you speak the affirmation, create a picture in your mind of what you want to happen. So, if you want to feel the power of your ancestors flow through you, imagine what that might look like and create an image. Combining visualization with affirmation adds extra oomph and sends a powerful message to the Universe.

- Enjoy the process. Affirmations are fun, and they really do work if you get into the habit of repeating them regularly.

Journal Exercise

Reflect upon the activities within this chapter. What have you learned about Ancestral Magic and how you can work with it? Think about the spells and rituals that you enjoyed the most. Why did they work so well? Perhaps they tapped into a particular skill set that is unique to you or your family? Now consider the spells that you struggled with. Why did you find them difficult? Is this something you could work on? For example, maybe you struggled saying the magical chants aloud and preferred to work in silence or write the words down.

   Look back at any notes you have made and highlight any successes. Believe in yourself and the power that lives within you. Write a list of all the ways you bring magic into the world, whether that's in the things you do for others, in your job, or within the family unit. Identify any new ways that you could have a positive influence on your surroundings, whether that's through spells and rituals, working with your ancestors, or doing something for your family and friends.

Summary

Ancestral Magic can help you find the real you. It can give you the confidence to truly blossom and find your own voice. By connecting with those who have gone before, you become rooted in the past and anchored by family values and strengths, which provides an innate sense of security. You belong, and that gives you power and identity and a spiritual place you can call home.

Even so, these tethers do not bind you; they are simply a safety net from which you can explore the world. They give you the freedom to grow in any direction, and when the winds of change come, they give you the flexibility you need to bend and stretch, without completely losing your footing because you know who you are and where you come from. You know that your ancestral guides are looking out for you. They are your spiritual support network, and you can call on them at any time when you need strength, guidance, or a little magical assistance. And the good news is, they've done a lot of the groundwork for you. They have faced similar challenges. They have loved and lost and lived, and while they don't know your life as it is today, they can provide valuable insight.

The gifts and talents that you share are a starting point, and they are also your familial superpowers; they can help you navigate your own path and find your true purpose. The ancestral karma too is helpful, for once you recognize inherited patterns of behavior you have the power to change them and to heal. Then there are the stories, the family folklore that you hold dear, and what they say about your ancestral line. Perhaps you come from a long line of dreamers, storytellers who see the wonder of the world around them, or maybe your ancestors were the jokers of the bunch, who liked to see the humor in every situation. The tales that you've been told alter your perspective on the world around you and can just as easily be tweaked to help you manifest positive change.

Getting to know your ancestors is an enlightening experience and you may be surprised by what you learn. Even if you're not a family history buff, just sharing stories and feeling that connection with the past can have a positive effect on how you view life. The rituals and suggestions within this book are a starting point, but the journey is never over. There is magic to be found in every family, treasures to be cherished throughout the generations, and lessons that can give you peace of mind and boost your personal power. There is strength at the heart of your ancestors. They are your clan, your tribe, the people who helped to shape you, and the place where it all began, so embrace Ancestral Magic and have fun getting acquainted.

"I am rooted to the past, I stand in the present, and I face the future."

Further Resources

If you would like to take your Ancestral Magic journey further and dig a little deeper into the medicine of the past, the following reading material will help. These books cover a range of approaches, from traditional native practices and shamanism, to traversing the spiritual realms to seek answers and find your true life purpose.

The books and websites listed below will prove helpful if you're interested in taking a practical approach and investigating your family history in more detail. They will guide you through the process of tracing your heritage and creating a family tree.

Books

Foor, Daniel, *Ancestral Medicine: Rituals for Personal and Family Healing,* Bear & Company, 2017

Gomes, Melissa, *Akashic Records: A Spiritual Journey to Accessing the Center of Your Universal Soul, Master Your Life Purpose, and Raise Your Vibrations*, independently published, 2021

Vaudoise, Mallorie, *Honoring Your Ancestors: A Guide to Ancestral Veneration,* Llewellyn Publications, 2019

Weatherup, Katie, *Practical Shamanism: A Guide for Walking in Both Worlds,* Hands Over Heart, 2006

Wigington, Patti, *Badass Ancestors: Finding Your Power with Ancestral Guides,* Llewellyn Publications, 2020

Chater, Kathy, *How to Trace Your Family Tree: Discover and Record Your Personal Roots and Heritage,* Lorenz Books, 2013

Pursley, Katiana, *Genealogy Organizer Book 6 Generations: Family History Book You Fill In,* independently published, 2022

Websites

www.ancestry.co.uk (UK)
www.ancestry.com (US)
www.findmypast.co.uk (UK)
www.findmypast.com (US)
www.ongenealogy.com (US)
www.familysearch.org

INDEX

Acknowledgments

I would like to thank the brilliant team at CICO Books, especially Kristine Pidkameny and Penny Craig, for their help in putting this book together. Also, thanks to Gina Rosas Moncada for the wonderful illustrations, which help to bring the subject matter to life. I would also like to say a special thank you to my mum. Her passion for family history and her amazing knowledge and skill at tracing our ancestors is what first gave me the idea for this book. Being able to see where I come from, and getting to know some of the colorful characters in my own family line, has inspired and empowered me. Thanks to her, and all the work she has done digging into the past, I know my roots, the gifts and talents I've inherited, and the stories and lessons that my ancestors can teach me, and that is something I will always treasure.